W9-BRY-600

books designed with giving in mind

The Ground Beef Cookbook
Cocktails & Hors d'Oeuvres
Salads & Casseroles
Kid's Party Book
Pressure Cooking
Food Processor Cookbook
Peanuts & Popcorn
Kid's Pets Book
Make It Ahead
   French Cooking
Soups & Stews
Crepes & Omelets
Microwave Cooking
Vegetable Cookbook

Kid's Arts and Crafts
Bread Baking
The Crockery Pot Cookbook
Kid's Garden Book
Classic Greek Cooking
The Compleat American
   Housewife 1776
Low Carbohydrate Cookbook
Kid's Cookbook
Italian
Cheese Guide & Cookbook
Miller's German
Quiche & Souffle
To My Daughter, With Love

Natural Foods
Chinese Vegetarian
The Jewish Cookbook
Working Couples
Mexican
Sunday Breakfast
Fisherman's Wharf Cookbook
Charcoal Cookbook
Ice Cream Cookbook
Blender Cookbook
The Wok, a Chinese Cookbook
Cast Iron Cookbook
Japanese Country
Fondue Cookbook

from nitty gritty productions

To my husband, Terry, for all his help in the kitchen,
Our son, Michael, and my Mom, the world's greatest cook.
A special thanks to my friends for sharing their recipes
and Jackie Walsh for her editing expertise.

Low Carbohydrate Cookbook

by
Joanne Waring Lindeman

Illustrated by Mike Nelson

© Copyright 1974
Nitty Gritty Productions
Concord, California

A Nitty Gritty Book*
Published by
Nitty Gritty Productions
P.O. Box 5457
Concord, California 94524

*Nitty Gritty Books - Trademark
Owned by Nitty Gritty Productions
Concord, California

ISBN 0-911954-30-9

Library of Congress Cataloging in Publication Data

Lindeman, Joanne Waring.
  Low carbohydrate cookbook.

    1. Low-carbohydrate diet. I. Title.
RM237.9.L55   641.5'638   74-5249
ISBN 0-911954-30-9

Library of Congress Catalog Card Number: 75-5249

TABLE OF CONTENTS

Dieting Without Boredom

After many years of trial and failure with dull, calorie counting diets, my husband and I discovered the remarkable Low Carbohydrate Diets and were elated to find that they worked wonders for us.

Because I love to cook and serve rich and interesting foods, my previous experience had been that I soon became bored on any diet. To avoid this and to make the new Low Carbohydrate Diet possible on a continuing basis, I started adapting my favorite recipes to fit the requirements of the diet, and created new ones which used the foods we like and which are normally not allowed on other diets. While doing this creative cooking, I lost 15 pounds. My husband reached his weight loss goal in no time at all. We ate large amounts of the things we like, didn't have to count calories and still lost weight.Who could ask for a better arrangement than that? Imagine a diet which allows such marvelous foods as steak with Bearnaise sauce, Roquefort dressing, avocados, barbecued ribs, sausage and eggs, whipped cream and even bourbon and water, Scotch and soda and dry martinis! Wines are also allowed but must be dry and taken in modest amounts.

There are, of course, a few restrictions on a Low Carbohydrate Diet. (Oh, well, nothing is perfect.) But I find it easier to remember the few things I can't have because I'm allowed large portions of the foods I can eat. I never feel hungry or deprived. You may find a few of your favorite goodies on the no-no list, but after a week of forgetting they exist and losing 5 or more pounds, you will see how easy it is to live without them. The thought of having bacon and eggs without toast was dreadful to me at first, but now I never think of the toast and appreciate the eggs even more.

It is helpful to have a Low Carbohydrate Diet book such as Dr. Atkins' Diet Revolution or The Drinking Man's Diet to help answer your dieting questions. And, a carbohydrate gram counter is a must. It makes menu planning easier and is a handy reference when dining out. A good multi-vitamin is recommended, while on this diet, to bolster your daily intake of Vitamin C, the B-complex vitamins or other nutrients. Check with your doctor as to the advisability of such a supplement.

Because I love to entertain, many of the recipes in this book are for company-type dishes, including lots of appetizers. They all are tasty, easy-to-prepare and proud-to-serve recipes. Most are my own adaptations, the rest are collected from friends and other Low Carbohydrate Dieters. They do not contain starch, sugar, flour, honey, pasta or fillers. The gram counts are approximate, but close enough for you to use with confidence.

Whether you are on a Low Carbohydrate Diet or not, I hope you will find these recipes interesting and delicious.

May your pounds come off where you want them.

Joanne Lindeman

Appetizers

Appetizers are my passion! They are fun to prepare and eat and they represent good times and lively conversation with close friends. It is wonderful to be able to diet and still consume these heavenly morsels.

Serve tasty little nibbles with cocktails, wine or diet drinks to whet the appetite. Always serve small portions, allowing 6 to 8 per person. They are meant to tease, never satisfy, especially if dinner is to follow.

If an appetizer is to be served hot—be sure it is hot! A warming tray is helpful. Keep fresh vegetables on crushed ice. Cheese is usually best served at room temperature. Have napkins and small plates available if needed.

These low carbohydrate taste-bud-teasers make excellent between meal snacks, too, when the "munchies" strike, and some are perfect as a luncheon dish. I hope all are interesting enough to stimulate your desire for more. Bon Appetit!

SEASONED ALMONDS

1 tbs. butter
2 cups whole blanched almonds
flavored salt
Parmesan cheese

6   Melt butter in small pan. Add almonds. Toss to coat well with butter. Bake in 300°F. oven about 30 minutes or until light brown. Stir often. Remove from oven. While hot, sprinkle with your choice of salt (garlic, onion, etc.) and/or Parmesan cheese. Cool. Store in an airtight jar.

Makes 2 cups   3 gm. per 12 nuts

DEVILED ALMONDS

1/4 cup butter
1/4 cup oil
1-1/2 cups almonds
1 tbs. celery salt
1/2 tsp. salt
1/8 tsp. cayenne
1/2 tsp. chili powder

7

Melt butter in skillet. Add oil and almonds. Cook, stirring, until nuts are golden. Drain. Blend remaining ingredients. Toss with nuts.

Makes 1-1/2 cups

12 gm. per recipe

CURRY CHEESE DIP

1 pkg. (8 oz.) cream cheese
1/2 cup sour cream
1-1/2 tsp. curry powder
1 tbs. lemon juice
seasoned salt

8

   Allow cheese to stand at room temperature to soften. Combine with sour cream. Beat until smooth. Add remaining ingredients. Mix well. Serve with seafood or Savory Meatballs, page 27.

Makes 2 cups   5 gm. per recipe

DILL DIP

2/3 cup sour cream
2/3 cup mayonnaise
1 tbs. finely chopped parsley
1 tbs. minced green onion
1 tsp. dill weed
1 tsp. Beau Monde Seasoning

9

Combine ingredients. Mix well. Chill. Serve with seafood or raw vegetables.

Makes about 1-1/2 cups

6 gm. per recipe

HERB-CURRY DIP

Serve with carrot and celery sticks, radishes, mushrooms, cauliflowerets, cucumber sticks, bell pepper strips, green onions and tomatoes.

1 cup mayonnaise
1/2 cup sour cream
1 tsp. mixed herbs
1/4 tsp. salt
1/8 tsp. curry powder
1 tbs. snipped parsley
1 tbs. grated onion
1-1/2 tsp. lemon juice
1/2 tsp. Worcestershire sauce
2 tsp. capers, drained

Combine all ingredients. Chill for 3 hours or overnight.

Makes about 1-3/4 cups

5.1 gm. total

CHEESE BALLS

Fabulous with cocktails!

8 oz. Roquefort or blue cheese	pinch cayenne pepper
5 tbs. softened butter	salt and pepper
1-1/2 tbs. minced chives	1 tsp. brandy
1 tbs. finely chopped almonds	2 tbs. minced parsley

Mash cheese in bowl with butter. Add chives, almonds, seasonings and brandy. Roll into balls 1/2 inch in diameter. Place parsley on plate. Roll balls in parsley to coat well. Chill. Dust with paprika. Serve with wooden picks.

Makes 24 balls   Trace gm. per ball

OLIVE-CHEESE BALLS

2 cups (8 oz.) grated sharp Cheddar cheese
1/4 cup minced ripe olives
2 tbs. soft butter
1/2 tsp. curry powder
1/2 tsp. garlic salt

12

　　　Combine ingredients. Blend until smooth. Chill. Roll into 1 inch balls. Spear with wooden picks.

Makes 20

Trace gm. per serving

AVOCADO BALLS

1 large ripe avocado
1/4 cup lemon juice
2 tsp. Worcestershire sauce
1/2 tsp. horseradish
Dash Tabasco sauce
2 tsp. soy sauce
2 tbs. mayonnaise

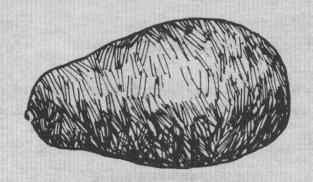

13

Cut avocado in half. Remove seed. Combine remaining ingredients. Blend well. Scoop small balls from avocado halves. Pour sauce over them. Chill thoroughly before serving.

2 servings   9.9 gm. per serving

CUCUMBER CANAPES

2 unpeeled cucumbers

1 pkg. (3 oz.) softened cream cheese

smoked salmon

capers for garnish

Cut cucumbers in 1/4 inch slices. Spread each with cream cheese. Top with small pieces of smoked salmon. Garnish with capers.

6 servings   Trace per piece

MELON BALLS

1 ripe cantaloupe   1/2 lb. Prosciutto

Cut melon in half. Remove seeds. With melon baller scoop out small balls. Trim fat from Prosciutto. Cut in strips. Wrap each melon ball with strip of ham. Secure with wooden pick.

4 servings   Trace gm. per serving

STUFFED ARTICHOKE BOTTOMS

1 jar (6 oz.) marinated artichoke bottoms
1/3 cup chopped toasted walnuts
1/2 cup canned shrimp, minced
pinch salt
1 bottle green goddess salad dressing

Drain artichokes. Pat dry with paper towel. Combine walnuts, shrimp, salt and enough creamy dressing to bind. Mound a heaping teaspoon shrimp mixture in hollow of each artichoke bottom.

4 servings

4.5 gm. per serving

ASPARAGUS SPEARS

1 lb. fresh asparagus
2 pkg. (3 oz. each) thinly sliced ham
1/2 cup grated Parmesan cheese

16   Snap tough stems from asparagus. Cook just until tender. Place asparagus spears on ham slices. Sprinkle with cheese. Roll up. Cut into bite-sized pieces. Fasten with wooden picks which have been soaked in water an hour to prevent charring. Broil ham pieces 5 inches from heat, 4 to 5 minutes.

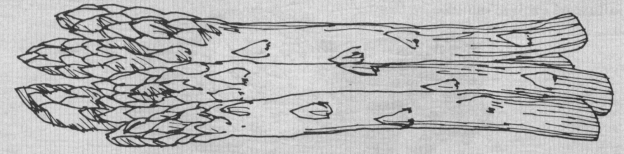

Makes about 60   Trace gm. per serving

ARTICHOKE HAM BITES

1 can (8-1/2 oz.) artichoke hearts
1/2 cup garlic Italian dressing
1 pkg. (6 oz.) smoked ham slices

Drain artichoke hearts. Cut in half. Marinate in dressing several hours. Drain. Cut ham slices in 1-1/2 inch strips. Wrap 1 strip around each artichoke half. Spear with wooden picks. Bake in 425°F. oven 10 minutes. Sprinkle with paprika.

Makes 20

5 gm. each

WATER CHESTNUTS WITH BACON

1 can (8-1/2 oz.) water chestnuts
1 lb. bacon
1/2 cup soy sauce

Cut chestnuts in half. Pour soy sauce over and stir. Marinate 2 hours. Drain. Cut bacon strips in thirds. Wrap each chestnut with bacon strip. Secure with wooden picks, which have been soaked in water 1 hour to prevent charring. Broil 6 inches from heat until brown. Turn. Broil until bacon is crispy.

Makes about 36   Trace gm. per serving

SALAMI ROLLS

2 pkg. (3 oz.) cream cheese
1 pkg. (8-1/2 oz.) sliced Italian salami

Allow cheese to stand at room temperature to soften. Place 1 teaspoon cheese on each slice of salami. Roll up. Secure with wooden picks which have been soaked in water an hour to prevent charring. Broil 5 inches from heat until salami is browned. Salami Rolls may be served without broiling. Garnish with parsley.

19

30 servings   1.6 gm. per serving

HAPPY HOUR MUSHROOMS

16 medium-sized fresh mushrooms
2 tbs. melted butter
1/4 cup soft butter
1 small garlic clove, mashed
5 tbs. shredded Jack cheese
2 tbs. dry red wine
1 tsp. soy sauce

Remove stems from mushrooms. Chop finely. Brush caps with melted butter. Blend soft butter with garlic. Add cheese. Mix well. Stir in wine, soy sauce and finely chopped stems to make a paste. Fill caps. Place on foil lined cookie sheet. Broil 5 inches from heat 3 minutes.

Makes 16   Trace gm. per serving

HAM STUFFED MUSHROOMS

4 dozen medium mushroom caps
3 tbs. soft butter
2 cups ground ham
1/2 cup sour cream
1/2 tsp. salt
1/4 tsp. pepper
grated Parmesan cheese
paprika

21

Wash mushrooms. Pat dry. Blend butter, ham, sour cream and seasonings. Stuff caps with mixture. Sprinkle with Parmesan. Dust with paprika. Heat 10 minutes in 350°F. oven. Serve immediately.

Makes 48   1.1 gm. per serving

ANN'S CRABBY MUSHROOMS

24 large mushrooms
1 can (8 oz.) king crabmeat
1/4 cup mayonnaise
1/3 cup finely minced black olives
2 tbs. chopped parsley
1 clove garlic, mashed
1/4 tsp. onion powder
1/2 cup (2 oz.) grated American or Jack cheese

Wash mushrooms. Pat dry. Remove stems. Drain and flake crabmeat. Mix with remaining ingredients. Stuff mushrooms with mixture. Place in buttered shallow baking dish. Bake in 400°F. oven 12 to 15 minutes. Sprinkle cheese on top. Place under broiler 2 to 3 minutes or until light brown. Serve immediately with napkins.

Makes 24   1 gm. per stuffed mushroom

6 hard-cooked eggs
1/2 tsp. Beau Monde Seasoning
1 tsp. curry powder
1/2 cup mayonnaise

Cut eggs in half lengthwise. Remove yolks. Mash with fork. Add remaining ingredients. Mix well. Fill egg whites with mixture, using pastry tube. Sprinkle with paprika. Garnish with parsley leaf on top of each egg.

23

Makes 12   Trace gm. per egg

ANTIPASTO

12 celery sticks
2 bunches green onions
1 bunch radishes
1 can (6 oz.) black olives
1 can (6 oz.) green olives
2 cans (2 oz.) flat anchovy fillets
1 can (4 oz.) sardines
2 jars (6 oz.) marinated artichoke hearts
1 jar (4 oz.) marinated mushrooms

1/4 lb. sliced salami
1/4 lb. sliced Provolone cheese
1/4 lb. thinly sliced Prosciutto
6 hard-cooked eggs
lettuce leaves
olive oil
wine vinegar
garlic salt

Chill all ingredients. Place lettuce leaves on large tray or individual plates. Arrange ingredients attractively on lettuce. Mix oil, vinegar and garlic salt to taste. Pass with antipasto.

6 servings

7.2 gm. per serving

24

BEEF SATÉ

Bamboo skewers
1 lb. sirloin of beef
1/3 cup roasted peanuts
2 tbs. lemon juice
1 tbs. brown Sugar Twin

1/4 tsp. Tabasco
1/2 tsp. ginger
1/4 cup soy sauce
1/2 cup water
1 clove garlic, mashed

25

Soak bamboo skewers in water for an hour to prevent charring. Trim fat from meat. Cut into 1/2 inch cubes. Chop peanuts fine. Combine with remaining ingredients. Simmer 10 minutes. Cool. Toss meat cubes with cooled peanut marinade. Allow to stand 1/2 hour. When ready to serve, thread 3 or 4 meat cubes on each bamboo skewer. Grill on hibachi or in broiler until nicely browned.

About 18 servings   1 gm. each

TERIYAKI TIDBITS

1 lb. boneless meat—chicken, steak or liver
1/3 cup soy sauce
2 tbs. extra dry Sherry
1 packet Sugar Twin
1/4 tsp. ground ginger
2 cloves mashed garlic

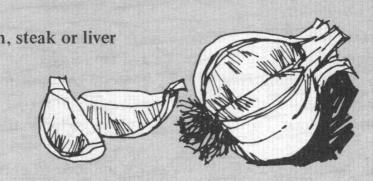

26

Cut meat into bite-sized pieces. Combine remaining ingredients. Pour over meat. Marinate, covered, in refrigerator 1 hour. Remove meat from marinade. Dry with paper towels. Broil 4 inches from heat until meat is no longer pink inside, about 5 minutes. Serve with green onions or water chestnuts. Pass wooden picks.

Makes about 60 tidbits   Trace gm. per serving

SAVORY MEAT BALLS

1 lb. pork sausage
1/2 tsp. sweet basil leaves
1/3 cup minced water chestnuts
paprika

Combine sausage, basil leaves and chestnuts. Mix well. Dip hands in cold water. Shape mixture into small meat balls, using a heaping teaspoonful for each. Place in baking dish. Sprinkle with paprika. Bake in 375°F. oven 15 minutes. Remove from oven. Drain off fat. Sprinkle with more paprika. Return to oven. Bake 15 minutes longer. Drain. Serve on wooden picks. Great with Curry-Cheese Dip, page 8.

Makes 4 dozen meat balls   Trace per serving

ANGEL WINGS

3 lbs. (about 15) chicken wings
1/2 cup Real Lemon, reconstituted lemon juice
1/2 cup salad oil
3 cloves garlic, crushed

28   Cut off and discard bony wing tips. Then divide each wing in half by cutting through joint with sharp knife. Place halves in shallow baking dish. Mix remaining ingredients. Pour over wings to cover. Refrigerate at least 4 hours or overnight. Remove wings from marinade. Place on broiler rack. Bake in 400°F. oven 45 minutes. Note: These are great for large parties. 15 lbs. will serve 40 guests. Make enough marinade to cover wings. Always use equal parts oil and Real Lemon. After baking, the wings can be frozen. When ready to use, bring to room temperature. Broil 3 to 4 minutes to heat thoroughly.

Makes about 30   Trace gm. per serving

CHOPPED CHICKEN LIVERS

1/2 lb. chicken livers
1 cup chicken broth
1/2 cup minced onion
2 tbs. butter
2 hard cooked eggs
2 tbs. mayonnaise
salt and pepper
1 tbs. chives

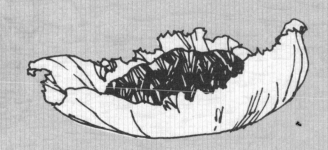

29

Place livers in small saucepan. Cover with broth. Bring to boil. Simmer 10 minutes. Drain. Cool. Chop very fine. Saute onion in butter, stirring until lightly browned. Chop eggs very fine. Blend livers, onion and eggs well to make a paste. Stir in mayonnaise. Add salt and pepper. Serve in lettuce cups. Also good served on ham slices.

4 servings   3 gm. per serving

BACON WRAPPED SHRIMP

1 lb. large green shrimp
1/4 cup olive oil
1/2 tsp. garlic powder
1 tsp. Beau Monde Seasoning
salt and pepper
1 tbs. wine vinegar
1/2 lb. bacon

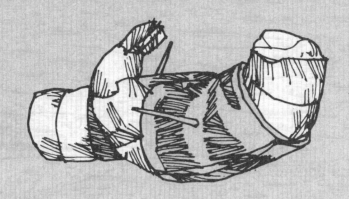

30

Shell and devein shrimp. Wash and pat dry. Combine oil, garlic powder, seasonings and vinegar. Pour over shrimp. Marinate 3 hours at room temperature. Slice bacon strips in thirds. Wrap each shrimp with bacon strip. Fasten with wooden picks which have been soaked in water an hour to prevent charring. Broil 5 inches from heat until bacon is crisp. Turn once or twice.

4 servings   Trace gm. per serving

MARINATED SHRIMP

2 lbs. green, unshelled shrimp
1 tbs. salt
1/2 cup chopped celery
2 bay leaves
2 Bermuda onions, sliced

2 tbs. capers
1 cup salad oil
1/2 cup wine vinegar
2 tsp. celery seed
dash Tabasco

Combine 2 quarts water, salt, celery and bay leaves in large kettle. Bring to boil. Simmer 10 minutes. Add shrimp. Bring to boil. Remove at once from heat. Allow to stand 5 minutes. Drain. Rinse shrimp in cold water. Peel and devein. Layer with onions and capers in medium bowl. Mix remaining ingredients. Pour over shrimp. Cover. Chill overnight. Serve in marinade, or drain, and spear with wooden picks.

8 servings

3 gm. per serving

SEVICHE

This recipe for pickled raw fish comes from Mexico.

1-1/2 lbs. lemon sole, sea bass, halibut
     or other firm white fish
1 cup lime juice
1/2 cup olive oil
1/4 cup minced onion
2 tbs. canned green chiles , minced
1/4 cup minced parsley

1 clove garlic, minced
1-1/2 tsp. salt
1 tsp. pepper
Dash Tabasco
1 tsp. fresh cilantro
     or Chinese parsley, chopped

    Cut fish in thin strips. Cover with lime juice. Chill 4 hours. Drain. Blend remaining ingredients, except cilantro. Toss with fish strips. Chill. Serve with chopped cilantro as garnish.

4 to 6 servings   25 gm. per recipe

CHICKEN GUMBO

1/4 cup butter
1 onion chopped
1 finely chopped bell pepper
1-1/2 cups cooked or canned okra
1 qt. chicken stock
2 cups cooked tomatoes
1 bay leaf
1 tbs. chopped parsley
1-1/2 cups cooked, diced chicken

Melt butter in saucepan. Saute onion, bell pepper and okra until golden brown. Stir in chicken stock, tomatoes and bay leaf. Simmer 45 minutes. Season to taste. Fifteen minutes before serving, add parsley and cooked chicken. Heat slowly to serving temperature.

6 servings   8.7 gm. per serving

FRESH MUSHROOM SOUP

1 lb. fresh mushrooms
1 bunch green onions
2 tbs. butter
salt and pepper
2 cans (10-1/2 oz.) beef broth
1 can water
1/2 cup dry white wine
1 cup whipping cream
2 egg yolks

Finely chop mushrooms and onions. (Use blender on "chop" setting, if available.) Saute in butter until tender. Season with salt and pepper. Add broth, water and wine. Simmer, covered, 1 hour. Combine cream and egg yolks. Add some of hot soup to cream-egg mixture, a little at a time. Stir heated mixture back into pot of soup. Bring to serving temperature. Do not allow to boil.

6 servings   3 gm. per serving

FRESH SPINACH SOUP

2 qts. chicken stock
1 lb. spinach
2 tbs. butter
3 eggs
2 tsp. lemon juice
salt and pepper
1/2 cup grated Parmesan
Baken-ets

Slowly heat broth in large pot. Wash spinach well. Cook in butter just until tender. Beat eggs with lemon juice, salt and pepper. Add a little hot stock. Blend. Add spinach to pot of hot broth. Stir in egg mixture until well blended. Add cheese and Baken-ets. Serve very hot.

8 servings   3 gm. per serving

Salads

Salads are many things to many people, but one thing they need not be is monotonous. A good salad provides an interesting, nutritious experience, and it's the ad-libber's greatest moment. Salads can be served pre-dinner, with the main course, following the main course (as is the custom in France), or as the main dish for a luncheon or light summer supper.

Greens of one kind or another are available the year around, so there's no end to the variety you can serve. Whatever is used, it must be fresh and cold. Warm, limp greens are unforgivable. They must be washed, dried and allowed to chill to a crisp before being served. The bowls or plates used for serving should also be chilled. Try putting salad forks in the freezer for a few minutes and bring them to the table, frosty cold, with the chilled salad. Who could resist? Getting greens well dried (and they must be dry in order to crisp properly) is a time consuming task unless you know this modern version of an old trick. After washing well, shake off excess water, and put greens in a large cloth bag. (I have a new pillowcase I keep just for this purpose.) Twist and knot the end or secure with a clothespin. Set the automatic washer on "spin dry" and drop in the bag of greens. In a second, you'll have the driest salad greens imaginable. Put the whole thing, bag and all, right in the refrigerator to chill until needed. Before automatic washers, women achieved the same effect by twirling the bag over their heads a few times to spin out the water . . . and that works, too!

Another do-ahead step in salad preparation is to prepare your vegetables such as celery, cucumbers, radishes, green onions, avocado, etc., and place them in the salad bowl. Pour on the amount of dressing you think your salad will need. Tear crisp salad greens and place on top. DO NOT TOSS. Cover with plastic wrap and refrigerate until needed. Remove plastic, toss and serve immediately, on chilled

plates. A quick squeeze of fresh lemon juice just before the last toss adds a nice fresh flavor to any salad.

I hope my salad-making hints prove helpful and the recipes enjoyable. Add your own innovations to what I've given you ... that's what makes salads delicious and fun to make.

CUCUMBER SOUR CREAM SALAD

Cool-as-a-cucumber really fits this warm weather favorite. Delicious with poached or grilled salmon. It's a perfect choice for a buffet supper any time of the year, because it adds contrast in flavor and texture to other foods.

3 cucumbers, thinly sliced
2 tbs. chopped chives
pepper
1 cup (1/2 pint) sour cream
9 bacon slices

Place cucumbers in bowl. Mix with chives, pepper to taste and sour cream. DO NOT SALT. Refrigerate for several hours. Cut bacon slices in thin crosswise strips. Saute until very crisp. Drain well on paper towels. Set aside. Just before serving, salt to taste. Place generous helpings on lettuce leaves. Top with bacon bits.

6 servings   2.6 gm. per serving

40

ALMOND PEPPER-RINGS

3 Bell peppers
1 pkg. (8 oz.) cream cheese
1/4 cup chopped dill pickle
2 hard-cooked eggs, chopped
salt and pepper
1/4 cup mayonnaise
1/2 cup toasted, chopped almonds
Iceberg lettuce
Classic French Dressing, page 68

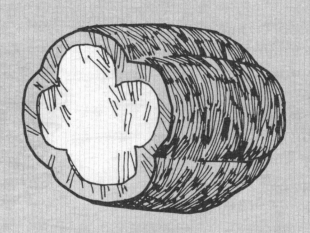

41

Cut slice from stem end of peppers. Remove ribs and seeds. Soften cheese. Add pickle, eggs, salt, pepper, mayonnaise and almonds. Mix well. Stuff peppers with mixture. Refrigerate overnight. When ready to serve, cut peppers crosswise into 1/2 inch slices. Place slices on lettuce lined salad plates. Serve with French dressing.

8 servings

4 gm. per serving

MARINATED MUSHROOM SALAD

1/2 lb. fresh, button mushrooms
1 sweet onion, thinly sliced
1/3 cup salad oil
1 clove garlic, minced
2 tbs. minced parsley
1/4 cup tarragon wine vinegar
1 drop Tabasco
1/2 tsp. salt
1 head Iceberg lettuce

42

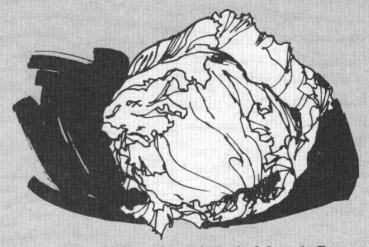

Rinse mushrooms and pat dry. Combine with onions in salad bowl. Pour on oil, garlic, parsley, vinegar, Tabasco and salt. Mix gently. Cover bowl. Marinate at least 4 hours. Just before serving, break cold, crisp lettuce into the bowl. Toss all together and serve immediately on well chilled salad plates.

6 servings   3 gm. per serving

TOMATOES ACAPULCO

These beautiful tomatoes will serve 2 for a luncheon salad, or 4 to 6 as a dinner salad.

2 ripe avocados
2 tbs. minced onion
1 tbs. lemon juice
salt
1 tbs. mayonnaise
2 drops Tabasco
2 tomatoes, sliced

Mash avocados. Stir in onion, lemon juice, salt, mayonnaise and Tabasco. Lay tomato slices on a bed of lettuce. Top with avocado mixture.

Makes 2 to 6 servings   3 gm. per recipe

NUTTY COLE SLAW

1/3 cup cream
1-1/2 tbs. white vinegar
1/2 tsp. seasoned salt
1/2 tsp. salt
1/4 tsp. pepper
1/2 tsp. ground tumeric

1/2 tsp. dry mustard
1 tbs. celery seed
1/4 cup finely chopped, salted peanuts
1/3 cup mayonnaise
1 medium head cabbage, shredded

Combine cream, vinegar, seasonings. Blend in mayonnaise. Stir in peanuts. Put cabbage in bowl. Make a well in center. Slowly pour in dressing, mixing in cabbage as you pour. Continue pouring and stirring until all cabbage is coated with dressing. Chill 30 minutes. Adjust seasonings, if needed.

6 servings

4.4 gms. per serving

STUFFED GREEN CHILES

This spicy salad goes well with broiled chicken and it's always a hit at brunch when served with an omelet or scrambled eggs.

2 cans (7 oz. each) Ortega green chiles
1 pkg. (8 oz.) cream cheese, softened
3 tbs. sour cream
garlic salt to taste
tomato slices

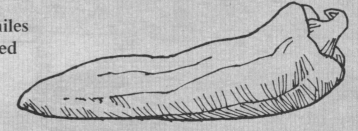

Wash and carefully remove seeds from chiles so they don't split on both sides. Pat dry with paper towels. Mix cream cheese, sour cream and garlic salt. Beat until smooth. Lay chiles flat and carefully spread with cheese mixture. Roll up lengthwise. Allow 2 for each serving. Place on bed of lettuce. Garnish with tomato slices.

6 servings   3.3 gm. per serving

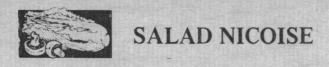

SALAD NICOISE

This pretty, classic salad is a favorite for many occasions. Serve with a tray of different kinds of cheeses for a satisfying meal.

DRESSING

1/2 cup olive oil
2 tbs. wine vinegar
1 tsp. salt
1/2 tsp. pepper
1 tsp. dry mustard
1 tbs. chopped chives
1 tbs. minced parsley

Shake ingredients together in a cruet. Shake again vigorously just before using.

1 pkg. (10 oz.) frozen green beans
1 head Boston lettuce
1 clove garlic
2 cans (7 oz. each) tuna, drained
1 onion, quartered and sliced

2 tomatoes, cut in wedges
2 hard-cooked eggs, quartered
1 can (2 oz.) rolled anchovy fillets, drained
1 can (4 oz.) pitted ripe olives
1 tbs. capers

Cook and drain green beans well. Toss with enough dressing to coat thoroughly. Wash and drain lettuce well. Tear into bite-sized pieces. Rub a large, shallow salad bowl with cut garlic. Line with torn lettuce. Unmold tuna in center of bowl. Carefully separate into chunks. Arrange separate mounds of green beans, onions, tomatoes and eggs in colorful groupings around tuna. Garnish with anchovies, olives and capers. Pour dressing over all when ready to serve. Toss at the table.

6 servings

5 gm. per serving

CHUNKY CHICKEN SALAD

2 tbs. white wine vinegar
1/3 cup oil
1 tsp. salt
1/4 tsp. pepper
1/2 tsp. crushed tarragon
2 cups cooked chicken, in chunks

1 cup thinly sliced mushrooms
1 thinly sliced green pepper
2 small tomatoes, cut in wedges
1 small cucumber, peeled and sliced
lettuce or other salad greens
1 hard-cooked egg yolk, sieved

48

Combine vinegar, oil, salt, pepper and tarragon in large mixing bowl. Add chicken, mushrooms and green pepper. Toss lightly. Cover tightly and marinate in refrigerator 1 hour or more. At serving time, add tomatoes and cucumber. Toss gently. Pile on lettuce leaves. Sprinkle with sieved yolk.

4 servings

5 gm. per serving

BACON-SPRINKLED CHICKEN SALAD

4 chicken breast halves, skinned
3/4 cup Green Goddess Dressing, page 71
1/2 lb. bacon
1 cup finely chopped celery

1 cup finely chopped romaine
1 cup finely chopped watercress
salt and pepper to taste

Cook chicken breasts. (Place in casserole with well fitting lid. Add a stalk of celery and some leaves, onion slices, cut up carrot, salt and pepper. Cover. Bake in 325°F. oven about 1 hour or until tender. It is not necessary to add any water, but there will be broth at the end of the cooking time which you will want to save for other recipes calling for broth or water.) Cool chicken and bone. Dice meat. Mix with dressing and chill. Cut bacon crosswise in narrow strips. Saute until very crisp. Drain well. Set aside. Add celery, romaine and watercress to chicken. Mix well. Season with salt and pepper. Line serving dish with lettuce leaves. Mound on salad. Sprinkle with bacon pieces. Serve at once.

49

6 servings

2 gm. per serving

CHICKEN SUPREME IN CANTALOUPE SHELLS

Low carbohydrate melons and chicken salad make a fantastic combination. Best of all with this one . . . you can eat the bowl!

4 cantaloupes
5 cups diced, cooked chicken
1 tsp. salt
1 tsp. curry powder
1 can (5 oz.) roasted, slivered almonds

1/4 cup chopped green onion
1 tsp. grated lemon rind
1/2 cup lemon juice
1 cup mayonnaise

Halve, peel and dice 1 cantaloupe to make 1-1/2 cups. Place chicken in large bowl. Sprinkle with salt and curry. Mix well. Add diced melon, almonds, onions and lemon rind. Pour on lemon juice. Mix gently. Cover. Refrigerate to chill until serving time. Cut remaining 3 cantaloupes in half. Scrape out seeds. Scallop or zig zag edges. Cover with plastic wrap and refrigerate. At serving time, fold mayonnaise into chicken mixture. Spoon into melon halves. Garnish with mint.

6 servings

8 gm. per serving

TOMATOES WITH CRABMEAT FILLING

4 large tomatoes
2 tbs. sour cream
2/3 cup mayonnaise
4 tsp. chopped capers
4 stalks celery, minced
1 can (7 oz.) king crabmeat
black olives
watercress

Scoop seeds and pulp from center of tomatoes. Turn upside down to drain well. Combine mayonnaise, sour cream, capers and celery in mixing bowl. Add crabmeat. Toss gently. Sprinkle inside of tomatoes with salt. Fill with crab mixture. Garnish with olives and watercress.

4 servings   3.6 gm. per serving

SEAFOOD FILLED ARTICHOKES

6 artichokes
1-1/2 cups mayonnaise
1-1/2 tbs. Worchestershire sauce
1 tbs. horseradish
1-1/2 tbs. lemon juice

1 tbs. salt
dash cayenne pepper
1 tbs. chopped chives or parsley
1 lb. cooked, deveined shrimp
1 lb. fresh crabmeat

52

Cook and cool artichokes. Spread leaves and remove choke. Chill. Blend mayonnaise, Worchestershire sauce, horseradish, lemon juice, salt, cayenne and chives. Chill. When ready to serve, toss half the dressing with shrimp and crabmeat. Fill artichokes with seafood mixture. Garnish with lemon slices. Pass remaining dressing.

6 servings

12.3 gms. per serving

COLD AND CRUNCHY MOLD

1 pkg. lime D-Zerta
1/2 cup hot water
1 can (10-1/2 oz.) cream of asparagus soup
1 tsp. vinegar
1/2 unpeeled cucumber, grated
1/2 cup chopped celery
1/2 cup mayonnaise
1 tsp. parsley
1 tsp. grated onion

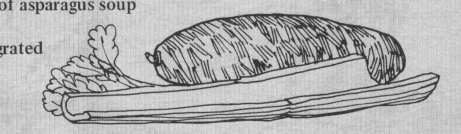

53

   Dissolve D-Zerta in hot water. Slowly blend into soup. Add vinegar. Whip until light. Add remaining ingredients. Pour into mold. Chill until firm. Unmold onto lettuce-lined serving plate. Garnish as desired.

6 servings   3.3 gm. per serving

Sauces and Dressings

A good sauce can be a culinary triumph, by turning a simple recipe into a gourmet's delight. An important thing to remember about sauces and dressings is that they should never dominate. A great chef will invariably use even his greatest creations sparingly.

Even when not counting carbohydrate grams, thickening is best achieved with egg yolks or by reduction. Sauces made with egg yolks will have a true rich flavor instead of the raw, starchy flavor of flour-thickened sauces.

When making a Hollandaise-type sauce, the results will be better if all ingredients are at room temperature. A double boiler is a necessity for making any sauce using egg yolks, as it eliminates the problem of curdling and makes the job

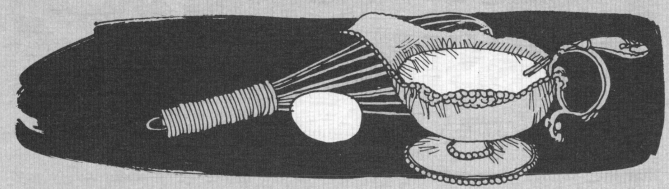

56

easier. A word of caution—be sure the water in the bottom pan does not boil or touch the pan containing the sauce ingredients. Either will allow the mixture to become too hot and overcook to the point of curdling. If, for some reason, a sauce does start to curdle, add an ice cube and beat vigorously with a wire whip until it is the consistency you want. If you don't own a wire whip you are missing a versatile piece of equipment which is extremely helpful when making smooth sauces and dressings.

MOCK HOLLANDAISE

When there's no time for the real thing, try this with artichokes.

1/2 cup mayonnaise
3 tbs. cream
1/4 tsp. salt
1 tbs. lemon juice

Mix mayonnaise, cream and salt in a measuring cup. Set the cup in saucepan filled with water. Heat for 5 minutes. Add lemon juice. Stir and serve.

Makes about 2/3 cup   1 gm. per recipe

HOLLANDAISE

Take pride and joy in a well made Hollandaise—the sauce of sauces. It's always a hit served on vegetables, poached eggs or fish. Serve warm, not hot!

1 cup (1/2 lb.) butter
3 egg yolks
1/4 cup warm water
2 tbs. lemon juice
1/4 tsp. salt
dash cayenne pepper

Melt butter and set aside. Combine egg yolks, warm water and lemon juice in top of double boiler. Beat with wire whip until blended. Set over hot, not boiling, water. Gradually add melted butter, beating constantly with wire whip. Continue to beat until mixture thickens slightly. Remove immediately from hot water. Serve, or set in cold water to prevent further cooking and curdling. Cover. Allow to stand at room temperature until needed. When ready to serve, set in hot water 5 to 10 minutes. Stir occasionally. If sauce should curdle, add 1 ice cube. Beat vigorously until smooth.

Note: Any leftover Hollandaise Sauce may be refrigerated up to 2 days. To reheat, first bring to room temperature. Place 2 tablespoons sauce in pan over very low heat. Beat until warm. Gradually add remaining sauce, 1 spoonful at a time. Beat well after each addition.

Makes 1-2/3 cups   2 gm. per recipe

SOUFFLED HOLLANDAISE

This is especially handy for stretching the basic sauce when serving a crowd. Great over asparagus or fish. Pop under the broiler until golden.

1-2/3 cups Hollandaise Sauce, page 58
3 egg whites

Prepare sauce. Just before serving, beat whites until stiff, but not dry. Fold into Hollandaise Sauce. Spoon over vegetables, eggs or fish. Place under hot broiler 3 to 4 minutes until golden. Serve immediately.

Makes about 3 cups   2 gm. per recipe

BEARNAISE SAUCE

The consistency of Hollandaise, but with a zingy flavor all its own to enhance broiled meats. Fantastic with steak!

1/2 cup tarragon vinegar
1/4 cup dry white wine
1 finely chopped shallot
1/2 tsp. dried tarragon leaves

3 egg yolks
1/2 cup (1 cube) butter
dash cayenne pepper

Combine vinegar, wine, shallot and tarragon in small saucepan. Bring to boil. Reduce heat. Simmer, uncovered, until liquid is reduced to 1/3 cup, about 8 minutes. Strain liquid into top of double boiler. Set over hot, not boiling water. With wire whip or beater, beat yolks into liquid, one at a time. Beat constantly until mixture thickens. Add butter, 1 tablespoon at a time. Beat well after each addition. Beat until all butter is used and sauce is thick and creamy.

Makes 1 cup   6 gm. per recipe

DRESDEN SAUCE

Serve this creamy horseradish sauce with fondue, fish, corned beef or cold sliced meat.

1 cup sour cream
1 tsp. Dijon mustard
1-1/2 tsp. horseradish
salt to taste

Mix ingredients until well blended. Cover and refrigerate.

Makes 1 cup

9 gm. per recipe

GREEK LEMON SAUCE

A favorite in Greece, served with roast lamb, this egg-thickened sauce is also extremely good over fish or chicken.

2 tbs. butter	3 tbs. lemon juice
1/2 tsp. salt	4 egg yolks
1 cup chicken broth	1 tbs. chopped parsley

Melt butter in top of double boiler over direct heat. Add salt. Gradually stir in broth and lemon juice. Cook over low heat, stirring constantly, until mixture boils. Place over hot, not boiling, water. Beat egg yolks in small bowl. Gradually beat in a small amount of hot mixture. Slowly beat back into mixture in double boiler. Stir constantly until thickened. Remove from heat. Stir in chopped parsley.

Makes about 1-1/2 cups   3.2 gm. per recipe

ANCHOVY MUSTARD SAUCE

This tangy sauce is delightful served as a dip for beef fondue or over broiled fish.

1 can (2 oz.) anchovy fillets
1 tbs. chopped chives
1 clove garlic, minced
1/3 cup salad oil
3 tbs. hot mustard
2 tbs. cider vinegar

Drain and chop anchovies. Combine with remaining ingredients. Chill until needed.

Makes 2/3 cup

3 gm. per recipe

64

TERIYAKI SAUCE

Use to marinate your favorite meats. A super dip for fondue or broiled meat.

1/2 cup soy sauce
1 clove garlic, minced
1 tbs. brown Sugar Twin
1/8 tsp. ground ginger
1/4 cup sake or dry sherry

Mix until blended. Refrigerate.

Makes about 3/4 cup

8 gm. per recipe

DIABLO SAUCE

For a festive treat, serve this hot and spicy sauce with scrambled, poached or baked eggs. Excellent with broiled hamburgers, too.

4 large fresh tomatoes
1 green pepper, chopped
1/2 onion, chopped
5 tbs. wine vinegar
2 tsp. dry mustard
2 tbs. horseradish

1 tsp. curry powder
1 tsp. oregano
1 tsp. garlic powder
1 tsp. salt
1 drop artificial sweetener
dash cayenne

Skin, seed and chop tomatoes. Saute green pepper and onion in small amount of oil in saucepan. Add remaining ingredients. Cook over medium heat, stirring, until thickened.

Makes about 2 cups   2.5 gm. per recipe

ONION BUTTER

An excellent seasoning for vegetables. Spread on steak, fish or chicken either before or after broiling.

2 tbs. dehydrated onion soup mix
1 cup (1/2 lb.) butter or margarine
1 tbs. minced chives or parsley

Blend ingredients thoroughly. Put in covered container. Store in refrigerator. Use as needed.

Makes 1-1/4 cups

5.2 gm. per recipe

CLASSIC FRENCH DRESSING

2/3 cup olive or vegetable oil
1/3 cup wine vinegar
1 clove garlic, mashed
1/4 tsp. paprika
1 tbs. Beau Monde Seasoning

Combine above ingredients in a pint-size, screw-top jar. Shake well to blend. Refrigerate until needed.

Makes 1 cup

5 gm. per recipe

CREAMY FRENCH DRESSING

2/3 cup olive or vegetable oil
1/3 cup vinegar
1 tsp. onion powder
1 tsp. garlic salt
1 tsp. paprika
2 tsp. crushed basil leaves
1 egg

Combine all ingredients in a bowl. Beat with rotary beater until well blended. Refrigerate until needed.

Makes 1-1/4 cups   3 gm. per recipe

BLUE HEAVEN DRESSING

My favorite Roquefort dressing. It's delicious for salads or as a dip for crisp, raw vegetables.

1 cup mayonnaise
1 cup sour cream
2 tbs. minced parsley
1 tbs. wine vinegar
1 tbs. lemon juice
1 tsp. garlic salt
1/2 tsp. Worchestershire sauce
2 oz. Roquefort cheese, crumbled

70

Combine all ingredients. Mix well in blender. Refrigerate several hours to blend flavors.

Makes 2-1/2 cups

9.7 gm. per recipe

GREEN GODDESS DRESSING

1/2 ripe avocado
1 onion, minced
1 clove garlic, minced
1/2 cup minced parsley
1 cup mayonnaise
3/4 cup sour cream
3 tbs. dry white wine
2 tbs. wine vinegar
1 tsp. dried tarragon leaves
1-1/2 tsp. lemon juice
1/2 tsp. salt

71

   Place all ingredients in blender. Run on medium speed until smooth. Cover and chill several hours to blend flavors.

Makes 2 cups   33 gm. per recipe

Meats

Consumer knowledge is important when buying meat. Make friends with your butcher and let him know you demand quality. Once you've established a good rapport, trust him. Ask questions and insist on getting your money's worth.

Beef, lamb, pork and veal are zero in carbohydrates and they're loaded with protein. They taste marvelous with or without sauces and stuffings, although these are nice when you want something special.

Menu planning with meat can be simple and exciting. Plan elaborate, fancy vegetables to accompany succulent roasts, steaks and chops. Sauced dishes such as stroganoff and scaloppine call for simple, lightly seasoned vegetables. Meat and vegetable casseroles that can be made ahead are great for busy days and many are outstanding enough to serve when entertaining.

This chapter includes family favorites and many company specialties. All are surprisingly quick and easy and I hope you will enjoy them.

MUSTARD STEAK

2 New York steaks
1/2 cup oil
2 cloves garlic, mashed
4 tsp. butter
2 tsp. Worchestershire sauce
2 tsp. dry mustard

Trim excess fat from steaks. Place in shallow baking dish. Combine oil and garlic. Pour over steaks. Marinate 1/2 hour. Broil 4 minutes on each side. Remove steaks to hot platter. Score with sharp knife. Rub in butter, Worchestershire and mustard. Spoon juices over steaks. Serve immediately.

2 servings   1.9 gm. per serving

STEAK DIANE

4 sirloin steaks, about 2 lbs. 1/2 in. thick
dry mustard
2 tbs. olive oil
1 tsp. freshly ground pepper
1/4 cup butter or margarine
1/2 tsp. salt

2 tbs. snipped chives
2 tbs. butter
1 tbs. Worchestershire sauce
2 tbs. lemon juice
1/4 cup brandy, warmed

Pound steaks to 1/4 inch thickness with meat mallet. Sprinkle each side of steaks with a little salt and 1/4 teaspoon dry mustard. Pound into meat. Drizzle on 1 tablespoon olive oil. Sprinkle with half the pepper. Press oil and pepper into steaks with back of spoon. Melt butter in large skillet. Stir in salt and chives. Saute 1 minute. Cook steaks, oil side down, 2 minutes. Rub remaining oil and pepper into second side of meat before turning. Turn. Saute 2 minutes more. Transfer to warm platter. Add remaining ingredients to pan juices. Blend well and heat. Ignite. Pour over steaks. Sprinkle with 2 tablespoons chopped parsley.

4 servings

Trace gm. per serving

FILETS WITH BEARNAISE CREAM SAUCE

BEARNAISE CREAM SAUCE

2 tbs. minced shallots
1 tbs. wine vinegar
1/4 tsp. tarragon
1/4 cup butter

1/4 lb. small mushrooms
1/2 cup whipping cream
2 egg yolks
dash lemon juice, cayenne

Combine shallots, vinegar and tarragon in small saucepan. Boil over medium heat, stirring until liquid is evaporated. Add butter and mushrooms (slice if large). Cook until lightly browned. Pour in 1/4 cup cream. Bring to boiling. Stir some of hot mixture into egg yolks. Return to saucepan. Cook briefly, stirring until slightly thickened. Stir in remaining cream if needed. Add dash lemon juice and cayenne to taste. Sauce can be reheated over hot, not simmering water.

6 beef filets, cut 1 inch thick
1 tbs. butter
6 tbs. dry sherry

Trim fat from steaks. Melt butter in skillet over high heat. Sear steaks on both sides until brown. Pour in sherry. Lower heat. Simmer 5 minutes for rare or 10 minutes for medium. Remove to warm platter. Spoon Bearnaise Cream Sauce over each steak. Serve at once.

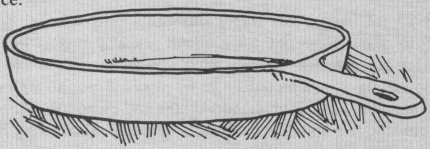

6 servings   1 gm. per serving

STEAK WITH MUSTARD CREAM

2-1/2 lb. top sirloin, 2 inch thick
1/4 cup dry vermouth
1-1/2 tbs. Dijon mustard
1/8 tsp. thyme
1/4 cup butter
1/4 cup whipping cream
watercress for garnish

Trim fat from steak. Blend vermouth, mustard and thyme in small saucepan. Heat to simmering. Set aside. Broil steak 2 inches below heat. Allow 6 to 8 minutes on each side for rare meat. Transfer steak to serving dish. Score top into diamonds about 1/2 inch deep to let juices flow. Salt well and keep warm. Return wine mixture to high heat. Add butter and cream. Boil rapidly until sauce is thick and golden. Stir constantly. Pour over steak. Slice meat, turning slices into sauce. Garnish and serve immediately.

4 servings   1 gm. per serving

BEEF STROGANOFF

2 lbs. top sirloin
1/2 cup (1 cube) butter
2 onions, thinly sliced
2 lbs. fresh mushrooms, sliced
2 tbs. tomato paste
2 cups sour cream
1-1/2 tsp. salt
1/2 tsp. pepper

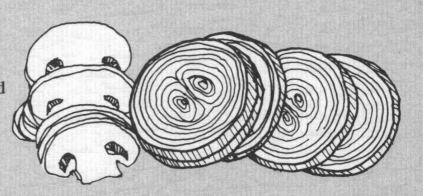

Cut beef in long thin strips. Melt 1/4 cup butter in skillet. Quickly saute beef until browned. Remove from skillet. Melt 2 tablespoons more butter in the same skillet. Saute onions 10 minutes. Remove from pan. Melt remaining butter. Saute mushrooms 5 minutes. Add tomato paste and sour cream. Return beef and onions to pan. Cover. Cook over low heat until meat is tender. Season with salt and pepper. Serve and enjoy.

6 servings   7.8 gm. per serving

FLANK STEAK PACIFIC

2 flank steaks
1 cup soy sauce
1 cup dry sherry
1/3 cup peanut oil
3 small garlic cloves, minced
1/2 tsp. ground ginger

Place steaks in shallow dish. Blend remaining ingredients. Pour over steaks. Marinate at least 4 hours. Turn occasionally. Grill 3 to 4 minutes on each side. Slice diagonally.

8 servings   2 gm. per serving

GREEN PEPPER STEAK

1 lb. top round steak
oil
1 clove garlic, crushed
2 onions, coarsely chopped
salt and pepper

1/2 tsp. curry powder
1 cup dry red wine
1 large green pepper
1 can (6 oz.) mushroom slices
tomato slices for garnish

81

Trim fat from meat. Cut into 1/2 inch strips. Brown well in 1 tablespoon oil with garlic. Add half of chopped onion, salt, pepper, curry powder and wine. Simmer, covered, 1 hour. Add more liquid if needed. Cut green pepper in thin strips. Brown with remaining onion in small amount of oil. Add to steak. Stir in mushrooms. Simmer 20 minutes more. Serve with tomato slices on top.

4 servings   9.1 gm. per serving

BARBECUED·CHUCK STEAK

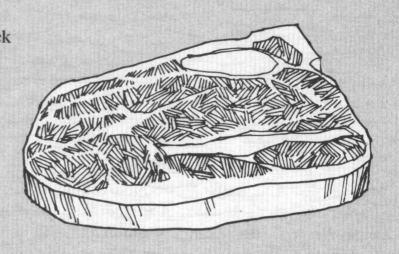

1 3-lb. chuck steak, 1-1/2 in. thick
1 tsp. Accent
1/3 cup wine vinegar
1/4 cup tomato sauce
2 tbs. oil
2 tbs. soy sauce
1 tbs. Worchestershire sauce
1 tsp. mustard
1 clove mashed garlic
salt and pepper

82

Sprinkle steak with Accent. Place in shallow pan. Combine remaining ingredients. Pour mixture over steak. Pierce meat several times with fork. Marinate 3 to 4 hours. Turn often. Place meat on grill or broiler pan. Broil 6 inches from heat, 15 minutes on each side. Baste several times with marinade.

6 servings   1.8 gm. per serving

BOMBAY BURGERS

2 tbs. butter
3 tbs. chopped green onion
1-1/2 lbs. ground round steak
3/4 cup mayonnaise
1 egg
3 tbs. prepared mustard
1 tbs. horseradish

1 tsp. salt
1/2 tsp. curry powder
1/2 tsp. cumin
1/2 cup peanuts
Worchestershire sauce
2 hard-cooked eggs, thinly sliced

83

Melt butter in small frying pan. Saute onion until tender. Combine with ground round, mayonnaise, egg, seasonings and peanuts. Form into 6 patties. Broil, pan broil or grill over hot coals. Cook about 5 minutes on each side. Sprinkle each patty with Worchestershire before turning. Remove to warm platter. Garnish with egg slices.

6 servings

Trace gm. per serving

PIZZA BURGERS

A pizza lover's delight and without the carbohydrates of a regular pizza.

1-1/2 lbs. ground beef
1/2 cup tomato sauce
1/4 cup chopped mushrooms

6 anchovy fillets, minced
1 tsp. garlic salt
1/4 tsp. pepper
6 thin slices Mozzarella cheese

Place beef, tomato sauce, mushrooms, anchovies, garlic salt and pepper in bowl. Mix thoroughly, but gently. Shape into 6 patties. Broil, pan broil or grill over hot coals. Cook 5 minutes on first side. Turn. Top with cheese slices. Continue cooking until done and cheese is melted.

6 servings

1.5 gm. per serving

NEW JOE'S SPECIAL

1 pkg. (10 oz.) frozen spinach
1 onion, chopped
1-1/2 lbs. ground round steak
salt and pepper to taste
5 eggs, well beaten

Cook spinach. Drain well. Press in sieve to remove all water. Saute ground round just until it loses its color. Stir in onion, spinach, salt and pepper. Add eggs. Scramble and serve.

6 servings   2.7 gm. per serving

CHILE RELLENOS CASSEROLE

2 cans (4 oz. each) green chiles
1 lb. ground beef
1/2 cup chopped onion
salt and pepper
1-1/2 cups (6 oz.) grated sharp Cheddar cheese
1 cup whipping cream

1/2 cup water
4 eggs, beaten
1/2 tsp. salt
pepper
several dashes Tabasco

86

Drain chiles. Cut in half, lengthwise. Remove seeds. Brown beef and onion. Drain off fat. Season mixture lightly with salt and pepper. Place half of chiles in 10 x 6 x 1-1/2 inch baking dish. Sprinkle with cheese. Top with meat mixture. Arrange remaining chiles over meat. Combine remaining ingredients. Beat until smooth. Pour over chiles. Bake in 350°F. oven 45 to 50 minutes or until knife inserted near center comes out clean. Sprinkle with a little grated cheese and dust with paprika, if desired. Cool 5 minutes before serving.

6 servings   2.9 gm. per serving

HAM AND ASPARAGUS GOURMET

1 (2 lb.) canned ham
2 pkg. (10 oz.) frozen asparagus _or_
32 fresh asparagus spears
2 tbs. butter
1/4 cup whipping cream

1 cup (1/2 pt.) sour cream
1 egg yolk, beaten
1 cup grated Muenster cheese
salt and pepper
1/3 cup grated Parmesan

87

Remove ham from can. Slice 1/4 inch thick. Cook asparagus 5 minutes. Drain well. Alternate slices of ham and asparagus in buttered 2-quart shallow baking dish. Melt butter. Gradually add cream and sour cream. Remove sauce from heat. Beat in egg yolk. Stir until sauce thickens. Add Muenster. Stir until smooth. Add salt and pepper. Spoon sauce over ham and asparagus. Sprinkle with Parmesan. Bake in 400°F. oven 20 to 25 minutes or until top is nicely browned.

6 servings   3.3 gm. per serving

CHOPPED VEAL STEAKS

Serve with Parmesan Tomatoes, page 167.

4 frozen chopped veal steaks
2 tbs. butter
salt and pepper
1/2 tsp. beef extract (Bovril)
1/2 cup whipping cream
1 tsp. minced parsley

88

Defrost steaks. Melt butter in skillet. Brown steaks. Add salt and pepper. Cook 5 minutes on each side. Remove to warm platter. Add beef extract to drippings in skillet. Stir in cream. Heat and serve over steaks. Sprinkle with parsley.

2 servings   Trace gm. per serving

QUICK CHUCK ROAST

1 4-lb. chuck roast, 3-in. thick
Kikkoman Soy Sauce

Trim excess fat from roast. Cover with soy sauce. Poke several times with fork on both sides. Marinate 24 hours. When ready to cook, place on rack 6 inches from hot coals. Barbecue 12 minutes on each side. Slice and serve.

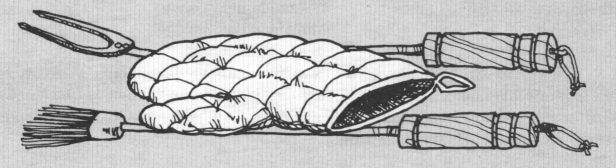

8 servings

Trace gm. per serving

BARBECUED SHORT RIBS

4 lbs. short ribs, cut in 3 inch lengths

Marinade:
1-1/2 cup salad oil
3/4 cup soy sauce
1/4 cup Worcestershire sauce
2 tbs. dry mustard
2 tsp. salt

2 tsp. pepper
1/2 cup wine vinegar
2 tsp. dried parsley flakes
1/3 cup lemon juice
2 cloves garlic, mashed

Trim excess fat from short ribs. Combine marinade ingredients. Pour over ribs. Refrigerate overnight. When ready to cook, place on grill 6 inches from medium-hot coals. Baste several times with marinade. Allow 20 to 30 minutes cooking time. Turn often. Do not overcook.

4 servings

4.5 gm. per serving

HONG KONG PORK CHOPS

8 large loin pork chops
salt, paprika
2 tbs. oil
1 medium onion, thinly sliced
1 tbs. soy sauce
1/4 cup dry Sherry
2 tbs. lemon juice

1 can (4 oz.) mushrooms, undrained
1/2 tsp. ground ginger
1/4 tsp. garlic powder
1/2 green pepper, chopped
1 can (4 oz.) water chestnuts
1 unpeeled lemon, thinly sliced

Sprinkle chops with salt and paprika. Brown in oil. Drain off fat. Cover with onion slices. Combine soy sauce, Sherry, lemon juice, mushrooms, ginger and garlic powder. Pour over chops. Cover skillet. Bake in 350°F. oven 45 minutes. Add green pepper, chestnuts and lemon slices. Bake 15 minutes longer. Serve with soy sauce.

8 servings   2.5 gm. per serving

WINE BARBECUED SPARERIBS

2 racks (6-8 lbs.) spareribs
salt and pepper
1 can (8 oz.) tomato sauce
3/4 cup dry red wine
3 cloves garlic, mashed
1 small onion, minced
2 tbs. brown Sugar Twin
2 tbs. wine vinegar

92

Place ribs in shallow pan. Roast in 400°F. oven 40 minutes. Cool. Cut ribs into individual pieces. Put in shallow pan. Combine remaining ingredients. Pour over ribs. Marinate 1 hour. Place spareribs 8 inches above coals. Grill 15 minutes each side. Brush with marinade every 10 minutes.

6 servings   6.1 gm. per serving

CORNED BEEF DINNER

4-5 lb. lean beef brisket
1 chopped onion
2 bay leaves
1/2 tsp. whole peppercorns
2 cloves garlic
1 leek
2 carrots
1 medium cabbage, cut in wedges

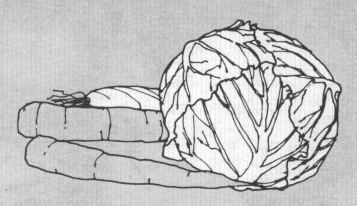

Wash brisket. Place in large kettle. Cover with water. Add onion, bay leaves, peppercorns and garlic. Bring to boil. Skim off foam. Lower heat. Simmer, covered, 4-1/2 hours or until tender. Add leek, carrots and cabbage wedges. Simmer, 15 to 20 minutes longer. Serve with Dresden Sauce, page 62.

8 servings   5 gm. per serving

Poultry

Sauced, stuffed, fried, baked, barbecued or broiled, poultry is always a favorite of the adventuresome cook. Its most important assets are versatility, low cost, high protein and zero carbohydrate count.

Chicken can be elegant, as in Chicken Kiev, or hearty and spicy in dishes such as Mexicali Chicken. Tempting chicken salads are a refreshing favorite for summertime eating, and what could be more satisfying and heartwarming than a big pot of homemade chicken soup?

Real economy comes with buying several chickens when they are on sale. Cut them up, wash well and pat dry. Separate the pieces for use in different meals. Bone and wrap the breasts for freezing. (With a sharp knife and just a little practice, boning a chicken breast is quite simple and fast). Wrap legs and thighs to be baked, broiled, fried or barbecued later, or add them to the soup pot. Save the wings, minus the small bony tips, in plastic bags until you are ready to make Angel

Wings. Collect the livers in a freezer container until you have enough for Chopped Chicken Livers or Chicken Liver Saute.

Many recipes call for chicken broth and none is better than that which you prepare yourself. To make really good chicken broth, put legs and thighs from 2 fresh or frozen chickens, wing tips, backs, necks, bones and trimmings left from boning the breasts, and any other scraps or skin left from cutting the chickens up, into a kettle. Add 1 quart water, 1 sliced carrot, 1 sliced celery stalk and leaves, 1 chopped onion and seasonings, if desired. Simmer until meat is tender, about 1 hour. When cool enough to handle, remove meat from bones. Use the cooked chicken in one of the salads in this book or dice it for soup or for a main dish such as Chicken Mornay On Broccoli.

Strain the stock. You should have about one quart. Chill and remove fat which congeals on top. Use for soup or in recipes calling for chicken broth. I often use this rich broth instead of the water called for in a recipe. It adds a nice flavor. A handy way of keeping the broth once you have it made, is to freeze it in

ice cube trays. Remove and store the frozen cubes in plastic bags or containers. When needed, defrost enough cubes to make the amount of broth called for in the recipe. After the first time, you will know how many cubes make 1 cup of broth.

   With just a little time and effort, chicken for several meals can be wrapped and ready in the freezer. Not a scrap has been wasted and you'll be serving boned chicken breasts at low sale prices! Take the savings and buy a really good bottle of wine for your next dinner party.

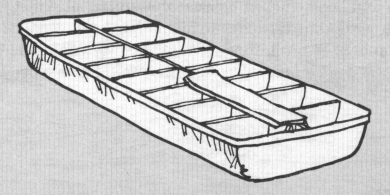

GARLIC CHICKEN

A simple, garlic-lovers treat. Unbelievably delicious!

4 chicken breast halves
1 cube (1/2 cup) butter
3 cloves garlic, crushed
2 bunches snipped parsley

Skin and bone chicken breasts. Melt butter in skillet. Add garlic. Brown breast halves in garlic butter, over medium-high heat. Reduce heat to medium. Cook 20-25 minutes or until done. Remove to warm platter. Keep warm in low oven. Add parsley to drippings in skillet. Mix well. Serve sauce over chicken.

4 servings   Trace gm. per serving

CHICKEN SCALOPPINE

8 chicken thighs or 4 chicken breast halves
2 tbs. butter
2 tbs. olive oil
1 clove garlic, mashed
2 cups sliced, fresh mushrooms
2 tbs. chopped parsley or chives

1/4 tsp. marjoram
1/4 tsp. thyme
1 tbs. lemon juice
3/4 cup dry white wine
2 tbs. pale dry Sherry

Skin and bone chicken. Pound between sheets of waxed paper to 1/4 inch thickness. Cut into 1 x 3 inch pieces. Sprinkle with salt. Heat butter and oil in skillet with garlic. Add chicken pieces. Brown slowly on both sides. Remove chicken. Discard garlic. Brown mushrooms quickly. Return chicken to skillet. Add remaining ingredients except Sherry. Cover. Simmer gently 30 minutes or until chicken is tender. Season to taste with salt and pepper. Stir in Sherry just before serving.

4 servings   5 gm. per serving

MUSHROOM STUFFED CHICKEN BREASTS

This is it, if you want an elegant dish for your next party!

1/2 lb. fresh mushrooms
12 chicken breast halves
1 tsp. lemon juice
1-1/2 tsp. salt
1/4 lb. Italian sausage links
3 tbs. finely minced celery
2 tbs. finely minced onion
3 tbs. finely minced parsley
2/3 cup dry Sherry
3 tbs. melted butter
1 cup chicken broth
1 cup (1/2 pint) sour cream

Wash mushrooms. Pat dry. Finely chop half of them. Slice the rest. Set aside. Bone breasts, but do not skin. Cut pockets in thickest part of each piece. Sprinkle with lemon juice and 1/2 teaspoon salt. Set aside. Chop sausage links fine. Saute in small skillet with celery and onion until crumbly. Combine sausage mixture, finely chopped mushrooms, 1 teaspoon salt, 1/3 cup Sherry and parsley. Mix well. Spoon stuffing into each breast "pocket". Secure with wooden picks. Brush with butter. Brown skin side only in hot skillet. Place in baking dish. Bake in 350°F. over 30 minutes. Combine broth with remaining 1/3 cup Sherry. Pour over chicken. Sprinkle sliced mushrooms around chicken. Bake 20 minutes longer. Baste often. Remove breasts to warm platter. Reduce juices in pan to 1 cup. Blend in sour cream. Heat slowly. Serve with chicken.

101

12 servings

3.1 gm. per serving

SUPREME OF CHICKEN WITH LEMON SAUCE

1 cup chicken stock
1 stalk celery
1 carrot
1 onion

4 chicken breast halves
1 egg yolk
1 tbs. lemon juice
1/4 cup heavy cream

102

Bring stock to boil in skillet. Slice vegetables. Add to boiling stock. Cover. Cook over low heat until vegetables are crisp-tender, about 5 minutes. Add chicken breasts. Poach, covered, over low heat 25 minutes, or until tender. Transfer chicken and vegetables to warm platter. Strain stock. Pour into saucepan and heat. Mix egg yolk with lemon juice. Remove stock from heat. Beat in egg yolk until creamy. Stir in cream. Salt and pepper to taste. Pour over chicken and vegetables. Serve immediately.

4 servings

4 gm. per serving

CHICKEN BREASTS MADEIRA

Perfect for a party buffet. A good Sherry can be used, but Madeira makes a difference worth trying. Use it if possible!

4 chicken breast halves
salt
paprika
3 tbs. butter

1-1/2 cups heavy cream
1/4 cup Madeira wine
12 button mushrooms, sliced

Remove skin from breast halves. Bone with sharp knife. Season with salt. Dust lightly with paprika. Melt 2 tablespoons butter in chafing dish over direct heat, or in frying pan on medium heat. Brown breasts lightly on all sides, about 15 minutes. Remove from pan. Add remaining butter and melt. Blend in 1 cup cream and Madeira. Return breasts to pan. Cook, uncovered, very slowly until tender, about 20 minutes. Stir in remaining cream and mushroom slices. Continue cooking very slowly 10 to 15 minutes longer.

4 servings

5.5 gm. per serving

CHICKEN KIEV

Pound pieces of breast with great care to avoid tearing.

8 chicken breast halves
1 cup soft butter
3 cloves garlic, crushed
3 tbs. minced parsley
3 tbs. snipped chives
salt, pepper
1 pkg. Baken-ets (pork rinds)
2 eggs
1 tbs. water
peanut oil for frying

Bone breasts. Blend butter, garlic, parsley and chives. Shape into 8 finger rolls 1-1/4 x 1-3/4 inches. Chill until very firm, using the freezer if time is in short supply. Place each breast between 2 sheets of waxed paper. Pound with wooden mallet until 1/8 inch thick. Be very careful not to split flesh. Sprinkle with salt and pepper. Place butter rolls in middle of each breast. Roll up. Fold ends in so butter is completely enclosed. Secure with wooden picks or fine string. Finely crush Baken-ets. Beat eggs with water. Dip 1 rolled breast at a time in egg mixture. Roll in crushed Baken-ets until completely covered. Allow to dry 10 minutes before frying. Pour enough oil to completely cover breasts into deep kettle. Heat to 360°. Fry breasts, 2 or 3 at a time, 6-10 minutes or until deep golden brown and done. Drain on paper towel. Keep warm. Remove picks or string before serving.

4-8 servings

Trace gm. per serving

MEXICALI CHICKEN

8 chicken breast halves
1 can (15 oz.) chili without beans
1 can (7 oz.) green chile salsa
1 bunch chopped green onions
1 can (3-1/2 oz.) pitted black olives, drained

1 tsp. salt
1 pkg (3 oz.) cream cheese, softened
1/2 lb. Jack cheese
1/2 lb. Cheddar cheese

Wash and salt chicken breasts. Place in casserole with a small amount of broth or water. If desired, add a few slices of carrot, celery, onion and a bit of parsley. Cover. Bake in a 325°F. oven about 45 minutes or until tender. Remove skin and bones from cooked chicken. Cut into large chunks. Place in oblong 4-quart baking dish. Combine chili, chile salsa, onion, olives, salt and cream cheese. Pour over the chicken pieces. Grate cheese. Sprinkle over chili mixture. Bake in 350°F. oven 30 minutes, or until thoroughly heated and bubbly. (If made ahead and refrigerated, it will need a longer time in the oven.) Add a tossed green salad with avocado balls for a great dinner.

6 servings   7.1 gm. per serving

CHICKEN ALMOND

If vegetables are sliced ahead of time, last minute preparation is easy.

6 chicken breast halves
3 tbs. peanut oil
1 pkg. (4 oz.) blanched almonds
1/2 lb. mushrooms, sliced
4 green onions, sliced
1 can (8-1/2 oz.) water chestnuts, sliced

1 unpeeled cucumber, thinly sliced
1/2 cup chicken stock
2 tsp. dry Sherry
1/4 tsp. powdered ginger
1 tsp. soy sauce
1 pkg. frozen Chinese pea pods

Skin and bone breast halves. Slice thin or cube. Add 1 tablespoon oil to wok or electric frying pan. Heat to 400° F. Add almonds. Cook, stirring, until lightly toasted, about 1 minute. Remove from pan and set aside. Add remaining oil. Cook chicken quickly, about 5 minutes. Add mushrooms, onions, water chestnuts and cucumber. Fry quickly. Add stock, Sherry, ginger and soy sauce. Heat 2 minutes, uncovered. Add pea pods. Stir until crisp and hot. Add almonds and serve.

6 servings   5.7 gm. per serving

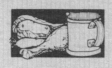

MAPLE BROILED CHICKEN

3 lb. frying chicken
1/2 cup butter
1 clove garlic
1/4 cup wine vinegar
2 tbs. Slim-ette Maple Syrup
1 tsp. salt, dash pepper
1/4 tsp. dry mustard
1/4 tsp. marjoram

Cut chicken into serving pieces. Wash and pat dry. Place skin side down in broiler pan. Melt butter in saucepan. Blend in remaining ingredients. Brush chicken with sauce. Place broiler pan 9 inches from heat. Broil 20 minutes. Turn skin side up. Brush with more sauce. Broil 20 minutes longer or until done. Baste frequently with sauce during last half of cooking.

4 servings   3 gm. per serving

3 lbs. chicken parts
2 tbs. butter
1 tbs. A-1 Sauce
1 cup (1/2 pint) sour cream
1 oz. blue cheese

Wash chicken parts. Pat dry. Place in casserole. Melt butter. Add A-1 Sauce. Pour over chicken. Blend sour cream into blue cheese. Spread over chicken parts. Bake 1-1/2 hours in 325°F. oven.

4 servings   2 gm. per serving

BAKED CHICKEN WITH MUSHROOMS

2 frying chickens
2 tsp. salt
1 tsp. celery seed
1/2 tsp. marjoram
1 can (8 oz.) mushrooms, undrained
1/4 cup toasted slivered almonds

110

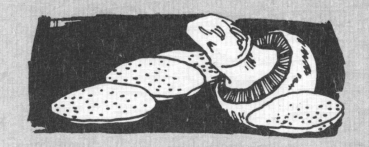

   Wash chicken well. Cut into serving pieces. Sprinkle with salt. Place skin side up in shallow baking dish. Sprinkle with celery seed and marjoram. Add liquid from mushrooms. Bake in 375°F. oven 30 minutes. Spoon pan juices over chicken occasionally. Add mushrooms. Sprinkle with almonds. Bake 25 minutes longer or until tender.

8 servings   1.2 gm. per serving

CHICKEN MORNAY ON BROCCOLI

1 pkg. (10-oz.) frozen broccoli
1/4 cup butter
1/2 cup chicken broth
1 cup (1/2 pt.) heavy cream
1 beaten egg yolk
1/2 cup dry white wine

salt, pepper to taste
1/8 tsp. Worchestershire sauce
1/2 cup grated Parmesan cheese
2 cups diced cooked chicken
chopped parsley

Cook broccoli just until barely tender. Drain well. Arrange in shallow 1-1/2 quart baking dish. Melt butter. Slowly stir in broth and cream. Remove from heat. Beat in egg yolk. Add wine, salt, pepper, Worchestershire sauce and 1/3 cup Parmesan. Arrange chicken on broccoli. Pour sauce over chicken. Sprinkle with remaining cheese. Bake in 425°F. oven 15 minutes or until hot and bubbly. Sprinkle with parsley.

4 servings

4 gm. per serving

BROILED CHICKEN SALAD

Cheese melts, but the salad stays cold! Also, delicious served very hot. For luncheon or supper, a tossed salad with French dressing completes the meal.

2 cups diced cooked chicken
1-1/2 cups diced celery
1/4 cup French dressing, page 68
salt, pepper to taste

1/2 cup mayonnaise
1/3 cup sour cream
1/4 cup slivered almonds, toasted
1 cup (4 oz.) grated Cheddar cheese

Marinate chicken and celery in French dressing 1 hour. Season with salt and pepper. Mix mayonnaise and sour cream. Add to chicken. Mix lightly. Sprinkle with almonds. Chill. (Note: If serving as a hot dish, complete without chilling). Fifteen minutes before serving, put salad in 4 individual, broiler-proof ramekins, shells or a 9 inch pie plate. Cover with cheese. Broil until cheese melts. (Salad will stay cold). Serve at once.

4 servings

4.2 gms. per serving

ROCK-CORNISH HENS - BROILED

For a special dinner party serve with Gourmet Beans, page 154.

2 Rock-Cornish Hens
1 pkg. blue-cheese salad dressing mix
2/3 cup salad oil
juice and rind of 1 lemon
2 tbs. water

Split hens in half. Place in shallow pan. Combine remaining ingredients. Pour over hens. Marinate 1 hour. Place marinated hens in broiler pan. Broil, skin side down, 5 inches from heat, 20 minutes. Turn. Broil 20 minutes longer or until done. Use all of marinade to baste often during cooking.

4 servings   1.2 gm. per serving

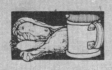

CHICKEN LIVER SAUTE

5 slices bacon
2 medium onions, chopped
1 lb. chicken livers
1 lb. fresh mushrooms
1/2 cup red wine
Dash dry Sherry
1/2 tsp. garlic powder
1/4 tsp. Accent
1/2 tsp. each oregano, sage, Italian seasoning

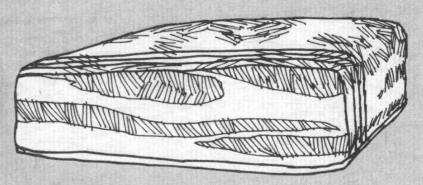

Dice bacon. Saute with onions until tender. Drain on paper towels. Pour off all but 3 tablespoons fat. Heat. Add livers. Saute 5 minutes. Add mushrooms. Saute 2 minutes. Add wine and seasonings. Cover. Simmer 8 minutes longer. Serve immediately.

6 servings   6.1 gms. per serving

WILD DUCK

2 wild ducks (about 1-1/4 lbs. each)
salt, pepper
soft butter
1 lemon
3 slices bacon
1/3 cup beer

1 tsp. orange marmalade
few dashes artificial sweetener
1 tbs. dry mustard
1/4 tsp. Accent
1 tsp. grated orange rind
dash red wine

115

Sprinkle ducks inside and out with salt and pepper. Rub skin with softened butter. Cut lemon in half. Tuck half in each cavity. Place ducks, breasts up, in roasting pan. Cut bacon strips in half. Lay pieces over breast of each bird. Bake in 450°F. oven 25 minutes or until lightly browned. Combine remaining ingredients in saucepan. Bring to boil, stirring constantly. Remove from heat. Reduce oven temperature to 425°F. Spoon sauce over ducks. Bake 25 minutes longer for rare or 45 minutes for medium.

2 servings   2 gm. per serving

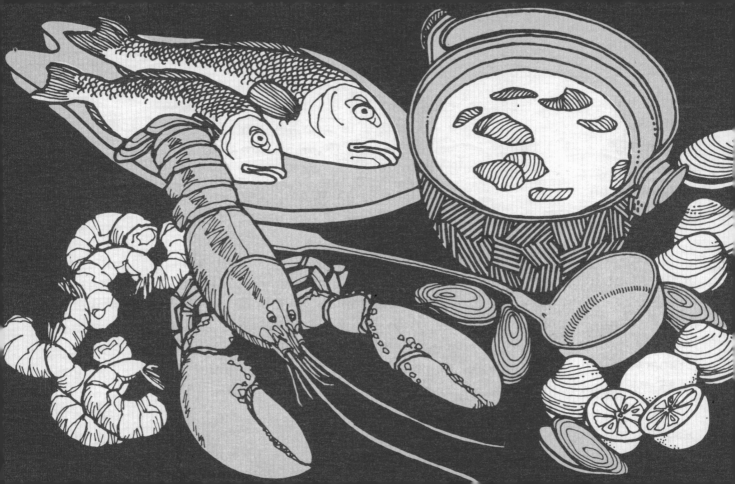

Seafood

When fish is your choice, I hope these recipes will please you. Gone are the days when the only way to fix fish was to fry it.

Seafood is a great source of high grade protein and is low in carbohydrates and in calories. While meat prices are soaring, serve more fish. Besides being nutritious your family and friends will enjoy the change.

On the following pages you will find tempting recipes which provide an extra touch to enhance the delicate flavor and texture of seafood.

Garnish is also extremely important, so pay special attention to it. A dash of paprika, a slice of lemon and a few sprigs of parsley will appeal to the eye as well as the appetite.

RED SNAPPER AMANDINE

1-1/2 lbs. red snapper fillets, or similar fish
1 cup dry white wine
2 eggs, well beaten
1 tsp. cream

salt and pepper
3 tbs. butter
3 tbs. oil

118   Place snapper fillets in a single layer in shallow pan. Add wine and marinate in refrigerator 1 hour or more. Turn once. Prepare Amandine Sauce as directed on page 119. Set aside. Remove fish from wine. Save marinade. Pat fillets dry. Dip in mixture of eggs and cream. Sprinkle with salt and pepper. Heat butter and oil in skillet. Brown fish quickly on one side. Turn carefully. Brown other side. Reduce heat. Add wine marinade. Cover. Simmer very gently for 5 minutes. Heat Amandine Sauce. Remove fish to heated platter. Pour on sauce. Serve immediately.

4 to 6 servings   Trace gm. per serving

AMANDINE SAUCE

1/2 cup butter
1/2 cup sliced or slivered almonds
2 tbs. lemon juice
1 tbs. chopped parsley
dash cayenne

　　Melt butter. Add almonds and saute until golden. Stir in lemon juice, parsley and cayenne. Heat until simmering. Pour over prepared red snapper fillets.

GRILLED TERIYAKI SALMON

4 salmon steaks, 1 inch thick
3/4 cup Kikkoman Soy Sauce or Teriyaki Sauce

Lay salmon steaks in shallow pan. Add soy sauce and marinate 2 to 4 hours. Grill 5 inches from coals for a total of 15 minutes. Turn every 4 minutes. Brush with marinade each time. Serve extra heated sauce with grilled salmon, if desired.

120

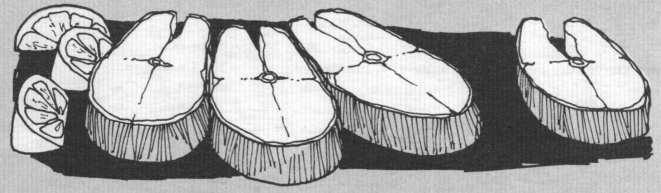

4 servings

1 gm. per serving

TROUT IN BACON

6 frozen trout
1/3 cup Worchestershire sauce
2 tbs. onion powder
1 tbs. lemon juice
2 tbs. salt
1 tsp. garlic powder
6 strips bacon

Defrost trout. Combine Worchestershire sauce, onion powder, lemon juice, salt and garlic powder. Brush trout inside and out with sauce mixture. Place in buttered baking dish. Score skin in 2 or 3 places. Strip with bacon. Bake in preheated 350°F. oven, 40 to 45 minutes or until fish flakes when tested with fork. Baste often with pan juices during baking.

6 servings   1.2 gm. per serving

FISH FILLETS BAKED IN SOUR CREAM

Pick your favorite fish for this succulent sauce.

1-1/2 lbs. fresh or frozen fish fillets
1 cup sour cream
1-1/2 tsp. Beau Monde Seasoning
1 tbs. soy sauce
1/4 tsp. horseradish
1 tbs. minced chives
paprika

Thaw fish if frozen. Arrange fillets in shallow baking dish. Combine sour cream, Beau Monde, soy sauce, horseradish and chives. Spread over fish. Sprinkle with paprika. Bake in 400°F. oven 25 to 30 minutes, or until fish flakes when tested.

4 servings   2 gm. per serving

REX SOLE WITH CHIVE-AND-BUTTER SAUCE

1-1/2 lbs. skinned Rex sole
1 egg
2 tbs. whipping cream
1/2 tsp. salt
1/2 cup butter
2 tbs. chives

Wipe fish with damp paper towel. Beat egg with cream and salt. Dip fish in mixture to coat both sides. Melt butter in skillet. When butter is foamy, add fish. Brown over medium heat. Turn. Continue cooking until well browned and fish flakes when tested with fork. Remove to warm platter. Add chives to butter in pan. Pour over fish. Garnish with lemon slices and parsley.

4 servings

1 gm. per serving

COD PIQUANT

1-1/2 lbs. cod fillets
1/3 cup Italian dressing
paprika
4 anchovy fillets
1 tbs. capers
4 lemon slices
parsley sprigs

124

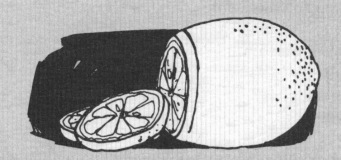

Marinate fish in dressing for 1 hour. Turn once. Sprinkle both sides with paprika. Broil 3 minutes on each side. Roll anchovy fillets around capers. Place on lemon slices. Use for garnish with parsley sprigs.

4 servings   Trace gm. per serving

TERRIFIC TURBOT

1-1/2 lbs. fresh turbot
3/4 cup dry white wine
2 tbs. lime juice
1 tsp. lemon juice
1/4 tsp. thyme
1/4 cup butter
6 green onions, sliced
1/4 cup Parmesan cheese

Place fish in baking dish. Mix wine, lime juice, lemon juice and thyme. Pour over fish. Dot with butter. Place onions on top. Sprinkle with parmesan cheese. Bake in 350°F. oven 20 minutes or until done.

4 servings   2 gm. per serving

BOUILLABAISSE

Try this traditional French fish stew. It's great for entertaining.

2 lbs. frozen flounder fillets, thawed
2 medium onions, sliced
1/3 cup olive oil
1 cup crabmeat
1 can (7-1/2 oz.) minced clams
12 fresh clams in shells
1 lb. frozen shrimp, thawed
2 cans (1 lb. each) tomatoes

1 bay leaf
1/2 cup chopped pimiento
1/4 cup chopped parsley
1 tsp. garlic powder
1/2 tsp. thyme
1/2 tsp. saffron
1 cup dry white wine

Cut flounder into "fingers". Saute onions in oil until golden. Add flounder, crabmeat, minced clams, clams in shells, shrimp, tomatoes and bay leaf. Bring to a boil. Cook 15 minutes. Stir in remaining ingredients, except wine. Turn heat very low. Add wine. Cover. Allow flavors to absorb 5 minutes. Serve in bowls.

8 servings   10.3 gm. per serving

SESAME SCALLOPS

These are divine served with Tomatoes Acapulco.

2 lbs. scallops
1/2 cup butter, melted
1/4 cup lemon juice
2 tsp. salt

1/4 tsp. pepper
1/4 lb. bacon
3/4 cup sesame seeds

Wash scallops in warm water. Drain and pat dry. Combine butter, lemon juice, salt and pepper in large bowl. Add scallops and toss to coat well. Allow to stand 1 hour. Stir occasionally. Cut bacon in half lengthwise, then across. Wrap marinated scallops with bacon strips. Roll in sesame seeds to coat all sides. Lay on oiled broiler rack. Broil 5 inches from heat, 3 minutes. Turn. Broil 3 to 4 minutes until bacon is crisp.

6 servings

5.1 gm. per serving

SCAMPI

2 lbs. large green shrimp
3 cloves garlic, minced
1 tsp. salt
1/4 tsp. pepper
1/4 cup olive oil
2 tbs. parsley, chopped

128

Shell and devein shrimp. Wash well and pat dry. Combine garlic, salt, pepper and oil. Arrange shrimp, single layer, in broiler pan. Brush well with oil mixture. Let stand a few hours to blend flavors. Broil slowly 5 to 7 minutes. Turn once. Sprinkle with parsley.

4 servings   4.5 gm. per serving

SEAFOOD FOO YUNG

Just as good with leftover roast beef, pork, lamb or chicken!

6 eggs, beaten
1 can (16 oz.) bean sprouts, drained
2 tbs. minced onion
1 tsp. salt
pepper
1 cup cooked crabmeat or shrimp
oil
soy sauce

Combine eggs, bean sprouts, onion, salt, pepper and seafood. Fry in small amounts of oil like pancakes. Serve with soy sauce.

4 servings   1.7 gm. per serving

CRAB IN SEA SHELLS

Beautiful and creamy. Serve with tossed salad . . . Yum!

1 pkg. (8oz.) cream cheese
1 tbs. cream
2 tbs. minced onion
130 1/2 tsp. horseradish
1/4 tsp. salt and pepper
1 can (7 oz.) crabmeat, drained
1/4 cup toasted almonds

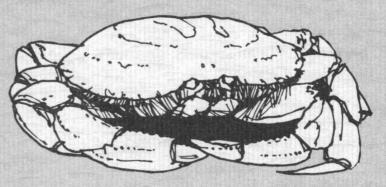

Allow cheese to soften a few minutes at room temperature. Slowly blend in cream. Add onion, horseradish, salt and pepper. Carefully stir in crabmeat. Spoon mixture into individual baking sea shells or casseroles. Sprinkle with almonds. Bake in 375°F. oven for 15 minutes. Serve immediately.

2 servings   9 gm. per serving

AVOCADOS STUFFED WITH CRAB

1 lb. crabmeat
2 tbs. butter
1 egg yolk
1 cup (1/2 pt.) whipping cream
salt and pepper

1/4 tsp. Worcestershire sauce
2 tbs. chopped pimiento
2 tbs. olives, chopped
3 ripe avocados
1/4 cup (1 oz.) grated Cheddar cheese

131

Remove cartilage from crabmeat. Melt butter. Mix egg yolk with cream. Blend into butter. Cook until thickened and smooth, stirring constantly. Add seasonings, pimiento, olives and crab. Cut avocados in half. Remove seeds. Fill centers with crab mixture. Sprinkle with cheese. Place in buttered 12 x 8 x 2 inch baking dish. Bake in 350°F. oven 20 to 25 minutes or until brown.

6 servings

6.3 gm. per serving

LOBSTER ALMONDINE

Serve with Green Beans Oriental for a real experience!

1 lb. cooked lobster meat
1 cup slivered blanched almonds
1/4 cup melted butter
1/2 tsp. garlic salt
dash pepper
2 tbs. chopped pimiento

Cut lobster meat into 1 inch pieces. Saute almonds in butter until lightly browned. Remove almonds. Add lobster. Saute until lightly browned. Add seasonings and almonds. Stir to mix well. Serve at once.

4 servings

7 gm. per serving

LOBSTER NEWBURG

How can anything this good not be fattening?

2 cups cubed lobster meat   3 egg yolks
2 tbs. butter   1/2 cup cream
1/4 cup Sherry   1/2 tsp. salt
2 tbs. brandy   dash cayenne and nutmeg

133

Saute lobster in butter 3 minutes. Add Sherry and brandy. Cook 1 minute longer. Beat egg yolks slightly. Blend in cream. Add to lobster. Cook over low heat until mixture thickens, stirring constantly. (Sauce will curdle if overcooked. If this happens, add 1 ice cube and stir constantly). Remove from heat immediately. Season with salt, cayenne and nutmeg.

6 servings   Trace gm. per serving

OYSTERS WITH PESTO

Quick and easy. Especially attractive served in their own shells.

12 small or 8 medium oysters
1/2 cup grated Parmesan cheese
3 tbs. minced parsley
1 tbs. crushed, dried basil
2 tbs. melted butter

Remove oysters from their shells. Scrub shells and save. Wash oysters and pat dry. Return to their shells. Mix cheese, parsley, basil and butter to make a paste. Pat mixture firmly over oysters. Broil 2 inches from heat until surface is browned, about 2 minutes. Serve in shells, garnished with lemon slices and parsley.

2 servings

3 gm. per serving

134

CLAMS BORDELAISE

The best you ever ate! A gourmet's delight and amazingly easy to prepare.

4 dozen small hardshell clams
1/4 cup butter
1/4 cup parsley, minced
2 cloves garlic, minced
2 cups chicken broth
1 cup dry white wine

Wash clams well. Heat butter in skillet. Add parsley and garlic. Saute 2 minutes. Pour in broth and wine. Bring to boil. Add clams. Cover. Steam until clams open, 5 to 10 minutes. To serve, arrange opened clams in individual bowls. Pour broth over clams. Serve immediately with extra melted butter for dipping.

4 servings   4.5 gm. per serving

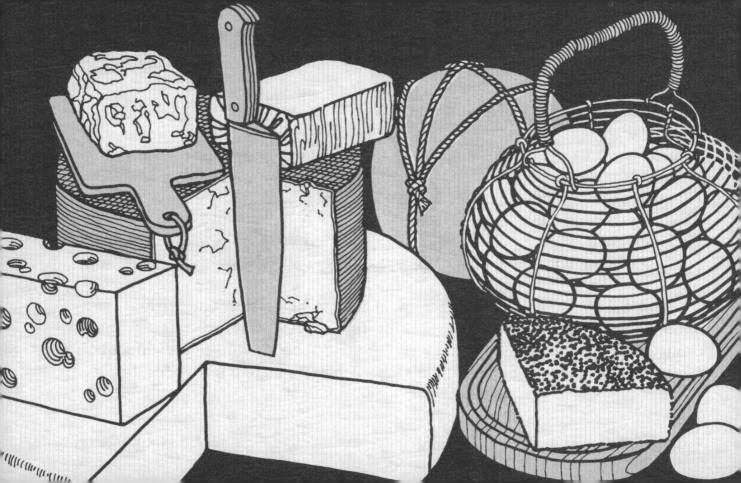

Eggs and Cheese

Eggs and cheese combine to make some of the most delectable dishes ever! Casseroles, omelets and souffles will satisfy your appetite any time of day.

Eggs are high in protein, zero in carbohydrates, low in calories and economical. Always buy the freshest U.S. Grade A or AA eggs, and never take home broken merchandise. Cracked shells might indicate contamination and certainly loss of freshness. So, inspect the contents and refuse to buy in any store where the eggs are not kept under refrigeration, no matter how short the holding time.

Storage is important at home, too. Keep eggs covered in the refrigerator. If you have unbroken yolks left from a recipe calling only for the whites, put them in

a container with a tight fitting lid. Cover with water and refrigerate. Drain off water and use. Whites should also be kept in a covered container, but without water. Use "leftover" eggs within three days and only in recipes which call for cooking them. Always cook eggs on low heat. High heat makes the protein tough and rubbery, and the yolks in hard cooked eggs will turn dark. When properly cooked, they stay bright yellow and look pretty when sliced. Have eggs at room temperature. Place in a saucepan and add cold water to cover by at least one inch. Cover pan. Bring to boil rapidly. Remove from heat and allow to stand, covered, 15 minutes. Cool promptly in cold water and remove shells as soon as eggs can be handled.

Cheese is another delicious source of protein. The next time you shop, take a good look at the wide variety of natural cheeses. There's a different one for almost every day of the year. Try some new ones. They make excellent substitutes for meat. Cheese in your diet will lead to happy, healthy adventuresome eating.

SUNNY SUNDAY EGGS

3/4 lb. bacon
1 bunch green onions
1 lb. fresh mushrooms, sliced
2 tbs. butter
12 eggs
salt and pepper
2 cups (8 oz.) shredded Mozzarella cheese

139

Dice bacon. Fry until crisp. Drain on paper towels. Pour off all but 2 tablespoons bacon drippings. Chop onions, tops and all. Saute until transparent. Remove and drain on paper towels. Melt butter in pan. Saute mushrooms. Beat eggs with salt and pepper. Add with bacon and onions to mushrooms and scramble. Serve on warm plates topped with shredded Mozzarella.

6 servings   1.5 gm. per serving

CALIFORNIA OMELET

Chunky Avocado Sauce, page 141
4 eggs, separated
1/4 cup water
3/4 tsp. salt
1/8 tsp. pepper

1 tbs. butter
2 slices pimiento cheese,
   cut diagonally in half
1/2 avocado, peeled and sliced
watercress

140

Prepare sauce. Beat egg whites with water and salt until stiff, but not dry. Beat yolks with pepper until thick and lemon colored. Fold into beaten whites. Melt butter in 10 inch frying pan. Pour in egg mixture. Level surface gently. Cook 5 minutes until puffy and light brown on bottom. Place in 325°F. oven 15 to 20 minutes or until knife inserted in center comes out clean. Place cheese over one half of omelet. Spoon Chunky Avocado Sauce over cheese. Tip skillet and slip spatula under omelet to loosen. Carefully fold in half. Slide onto heated platter. Garnish with avocado slices and watercress. Serve with sausage or bacon and sliced tomatoes.

2 servings
4 gm. per serving

CHUNKY AVOCADO SAUCE

1/2 avocado
1 tsp. lemon juice
1/2 tsp. green taco sauce *or* chili powder
1 tsp. minced onion

   Peel and dice avocado. Combine with remaining ingredients.

141

HUEVOS DIABLO

These Spanish eggs are festive for breakfast, brunch or a luncheon. Very pretty garnished with avocado slices.

Diablo Sauce, page 66
8 eggs
1 tsp. salt
2 tbs. butter
2 cups (8 oz.) Cheddar cheese, grated

142

Prepare sauce. Beat eggs until yolks and whites are well mixed. Add salt. Beat again. Melt butter in large frying pan. Pour in eggs. Scramble, until barely set. Sprinkle with cheese. Cover. Turn off heat. Allow to stand until cheese is melted. Serve with Diablo Sauce.

4 servings   1.5 gm. per serving

EGGS A LA RUSSE

These classic eggs are easy to prepare. They may be served for lunch or as an appetizer.

1/2 cup oil	shredded lettuce
3 tbs. wine vinegar	6 hard-cooked eggs
1 tsp. salt	12 flat anchovy fillets
1/2 tsp. pepper	capers
1/2 tsp. garlic salt	pimiento strips

Combine oil, vinegar, salt, pepper and garlic salt in screw top jar. Shake well. Chill for several hours. When ready to serve, arrange shredded lettuce on salad plates. Cut eggs in half. Lay 2 halves, yolks down, on each plate. Place an anchovy fillet across each egg. Top with a few capers and pimiento strips. Pour dressing over eggs.

6 servings   Trace gm. per serving

PERFECT 3-EGG OMELETS

The trick for making a perfect omelet is to keep the actual cooking time to no more than 60 seconds, and have the fillings hot! When making several omelets, wipe pan with paper towel between each one.

3 eggs at room temperature   1/4 tsp. salt   dash pepper   1 tbs. butter

In a small bowl thoroughly beat eggs, salt and pepper for 30 seconds. Melt butter in omelet pan or 8 inch frying pan over highest heat. As butter melts tilt pan to coat bottom and sides with butter. When foaming ceases and before butter starts to turn color (1-2 minutes) pour eggs into pan. Wait 5 seconds for eggs to partially set on bottom. Lower heat. Start shaking pan back and forth. Continue to shake pan a few seconds longer. Without piercing bottom layer of cooked omelet, stir uncooked egg with back of a spoon until it forms soft custard, about 40 seconds. Add 1/4 cup hot filling. Fold omelet over filling and fold over again. Serve at once on heated plate.

2 servings   1 gm. per serving

OMELET FILLINGS

Use 1/4 cup of any of the following fillings for each omelet.

1. Mushrooms sauteed in Sherry
2. Avocado slices marinated in French dressing
3. Sour cream with chives or bacon
4. Sauteed mushrooms, green pepper and onion
5. Grated cheese
6. Cooked and chopped spinach or asparagus
7. Cooked, chopped and sauteed chicken livers, ham, chicken, shrimp, oysters or crab

SPINACH SOUFFLE WEDGES

2/3 cup cream
1 egg yolk
3 tbs. butter
1/4 tsp. salt
1/4 tsp. nutmeg
2-1/2 cups (large bunch) finely chopped spinach
2 green onions, finely chopped
1/4 cup chopped parsley
1 cup (4 oz.) grated Swiss cheese
4 eggs
1/8 tsp. cream of tartar

Combine cream and egg yolk. Melt butter in medium saucepan. Remove from heat. Gradually blend in egg–cream mixture. Return to heat. Stir until sauce thickens. Stir in salt and nutmeg. Add spinach, onions and parsley. Simmer

uncovered 3 minutes. Stir in cheese. Remove from heat. Separate eggs. Put whites in large bowl. With spoon, beat yolks, one at a time, directly into spinach mixture. (This much of the recipe may be prepared ahead). Beat whites with cream of tartar until stiff, but not dry. Gently fold spinach mixture into beaten whites. Turn into buttered 10 inch round casserole, baking pan or fry pan with 2 inch sides. Smooth top. Bake in 350°F. oven 25 to 30 minutes or until knife inserted near center comes out clean. Cut in wedges. Serve at once.

147

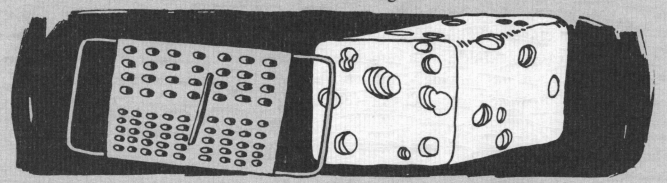

6 servings   3.6 gm. per serving

CHEESE AND SAUSAGE CUSTARD

1 pkg. (8 oz.) Brown 'N Serve Sausages
6 eggs
1/2 cup whipping cream
salt and pepper
1 tbs. minced chives and parsley
1 cup (4 oz.) grated Cheddar or Tillamook cheese

148

Slice sausages diagonally and brown in frying pan. Beat eggs, cream, salt, pepper and chives together. Sprinkle half of grated cheese over sausages. Pour egg mixture on top. Sprinkle with remaining cheese. Cook, uncovered, over low heat (200°-250°) without stirring, until set, about 25 minutes. Place under hot broiler until nicely browned on top. Cut in wedges to serve.

4 servings   Trace gm. per serving

MUSHROOM CHEESE CASSEROLE

Make one day—bake the next!

1/2 lb. mushrooms, sliced
1 tbs. butter
8 slices bacon, cut in half
2 cups (8 oz.) Swiss cheese, grated
1 cup grated Parmesan cheese
3 eggs, well beaten

1 cup (1/2 pint) whipping cream
1 cup milk
1 tsp. salt
1 tbs. minced chives
1/2 tsp. nutmeg
dash cayenne

Saute mushrooms in butter. Remove from pan. Fry bacon. Drain on towels. Sprinkle on bottom of 1-1/2 quart baking dish. Combine cheeses, eggs, cream, milk, salt, chives, nutmeg and cayenne. Pour over bacon. Arrange sauteed mushrooms on top. Bake in 350°F. oven 35 minutes, or until knife inserted in center comes out clean.

6 servings   4.3 gm. per serving

Vegetables

One of the most appreciated facts of Low Carbohydrate dieting is that it permits menu selection without the compromises of calorie-counting diets. Allow good judgment to prevail and select well balanced daily menus of low carbohydrate foods, including a variety of vegetables. It is best to avoid beets, beans (except wax and green), corn, peas, potatoes and yams because of their high gram count.

Cook vegetables quickly. Their color and flavor are best when cooked "crisp tender." Those served with richly sauced entrees should be prepared as simply as possible. Serve fancier ones with roasts, steak and other broiled offerings.

Always select the freshest vegetables of the season, for flavor and economy's sake, and try a new one occasionally. Buy in amounts you can use promptly while they're at their peak of goodness. Watch market ads for frozen vegetable specials.

I hope my recipes will add pleasure and variety to your diet.

ASPARAGUS VENETIAN

2 lbs. fresh asparagus*
1/3 cup Onion Butter, page 67
1 cup diced Mozzarella cheese
2 tbs. grated Parmesan cheese

152   Cook and drain asparagus. Arrange in 8 inch baking dish. Melt Onion Butter. Drizzle over asparagus. Cover with Mozzarella. Sprinkle with Parmesan. Bake 10 minutes or until cheese melts.

*If fresh asparagus is not available, use 2 packages frozen asparagus.

6 servings   4.6 gm. per serving

STIR-FRY ASPARAGUS

1-1/2 lbs. fresh asparagus
2 tbs. garlic flavored oil
1 tsp. soy sauce
1 tsp. lemon juice

Wash asparagus. Snap off tough ends. Cut off tips. Cut remaining stalks in 1/4 inch diagonal slices. Heat a heavy skillet. Add oil. Saute asparagus, stirring constantly, until it starts to brown. Cover. Cook 2 to 3 minutes. Stir in soy sauce and lemon juice. Serve at once.

4 servings

4 gm. per serving

GOURMET BEANS

2 pkgs. (10 oz. each) frozen cut green beans
1 pkg. (3 oz.) softened cream cheese
1/4 cup sour cream
2 tbs. cream
1/4 cup chopped walnuts
1/4 tsp. Worcestershire sauce
1/4 tsp. salt

154

Cook frozen beans according to package directions. Blend cream cheese and sour cream in small saucepan. Set saucepan in larger pan containing a small amount of boiling water. Stir cream mixture until heated. Add nuts, Worcestershire and salt. Mixture should be of pouring consistency. Add more cream if needed. Drain beans. Place in serving dish. Pour hot cream sauce over beans. Serve immediately.

6 servings   5.6 gm. per serving

FRENCH-CUT BEANS IN CREAM

3 pkgs. (10 oz. each) frozen French-cut green beans
1 tsp. salt
2 tbs. melted butter
1 cup (1/2 pt.) whipping cream
1/2 tsp. dried mint

155

Place beans in small amount of boiling salted water. Cook until tender. Drain. Put back in pan with butter. Toss to coat well. Add cream. Mix gently. Sprinkle with mint.

8 servings   6.6 gm. per serving

GREEN BEANS ORIENTAL

1 pkg. (10 oz.) frozen French-cut green beans
1 medium onion
2 tsp. oil
1 tbs. soy sauce
1/2 lb. fresh bean sprouts (more if you like)

156

Cook beans according to package directions. Drain. Set aside. Chop onion fine. Saute in oil, over low heat, until golden. Stir in soy sauce. Add bean sprouts and beans. Heat, stirring constantly, until thoroughly heated.

6 servings   **4.6 gm. per serving**

COMPANY BROCCOLI

2 pkg. (10 oz. each) frozen broccoli spears
1 cup (1/2 pt.) sour cream
1/2 cup (2 oz.) grated Cheddar cheese
1 tbs. lemon juice
1/2 tsp. grated lemon rind
salt and pepper
paprika

Cook broccoli according to package directions. Drain well. Place in shallow baking dish. Combine remaining ingredients. Spoon over broccoli. Sprinkle with paprika. Bake in 350°F. oven 20 minutes.

6 servings   4.1 gm. per serving

CARAWAY CABBAGE

Serve with sauteed sausages.

8 cups cabbage in 1/4 inch shreds
2 eggs, slightly beaten
1 cup half-and-half
1/2 tsp. salt
pepper
1-2 tsp. caraway seeds.

158

Cover cabbage with ice water. Chill 1 hour. Drain. Cover with lightly salted, boiling water. Simmer 5 minutes. Drain well. Put in buttered shallow 2 quart baking dish. Combine eggs, cream, salt, pepper and caraway seeds. Pour over cabbage. Bake in 350°F. oven 30 minutes or until custard is set.

6 servings   7.3 gm. per serving

GLAZED CARROTS

1-1/2 lbs. carrots
1 cup water
1 tsp. salt
1/3 cup dry Sherry
1/4 cup Sugar Twin
2 tbs. butter
1 tbs. chopped mint or parsley

Scrape carrots. Slice diagonally. Place in saucepan. Add water, salt, Sherry, Sugar Twin and butter. Steam, tightly covered, 15 to 20 minutes. Reduce heat. Remove cover. Continue cooking 5 minutes more. Stir frequently. Toss with mint or parsley just before serving.

6 servings   4.2 gm. per serving

CELERY PARMIGIANA

Celery never looked or tasted so good!

6 slices bacon
4 cups sliced celery
1/4 cup chopped onion
1 clove garlic, minced

1 cup water
1 tsp. salt
2 tomatoes, peeled and chopped
1 cup grated Parmesan cheese

Fry bacon in skillet until crisp. Drain, crumble and set aside. Pour fat from skillet. Add celery, onion, garlic, water and salt. Cover. Simmer 20 minutes or until celery is tender. Drain. Place in 1-1/2 quart casserole. Top with crumbled bacon and chopped tomatoes. Sprinkle with Parmesan. Bake in 350°F. oven 15 to 20 minutes.

6 servings

7.3 gm. per serving

BAKED EGGPLANT

1 medium eggplant
mayonnaise
3/4 cup grated Parmesan cheese
paprika
parsley

161

    Cut eggplant in 1/2 inch thick slices. Lightly spread mayonnaise on one side of each slice. Coat with cheese. Turn. Spread second side with mayonnaise. Coat with more cheese. Arrange slices in single layer in shallow pan. Sprinkle with paprika and parsley. Bake in 425°F. oven until brown and tender, about 15 minutes. Turn once to brown both sides.

4 servings   5 gm. per serving

MUSHROOMS AU GRATIN

Great with steak! Can be made ahead and baked just before serving.

1 lb. fresh mushrooms
2 tbs. butter
1/3 cup sour cream
1 egg yolk

salt and pepper
1/4 cup finely chopped parsley
1/2 cup (2 oz.) grated Swiss cheese

Slice mushrooms 1/4 inch thick. Heat butter in large skillet. Saute mushrooms until lightly browned. Simmer 2 minutes. Blend sour cream, egg yolk, salt and pepper until smooth. Add to mushrooms. Heat, stirring constantly, until blended. Remove from heat. Pour into a shallow baking pan. Sprinkle with parsley and cheese. Before serving, place uncovered in 425°F. oven 10 minutes or until mushrooms are heated and cheese is melted.

4 servings   4 gm. per serving

MUSHROOMS WITH PATÉ

1 lb. fresh mushrooms
3 tbs. butter
1 egg yolk
1/2 tsp. salt
1/2 tsp. tarragon

1 clove garlic, mashed
1/4 cup sour cream
1 cup (4 oz.) grated Swiss cheese
2 tbs. minced parsley
1 can (2-1/2 oz.) paté, chilled

163

Wash mushrooms. Slice if large, quarter if small. Melt butter in large skillet. Add mushrooms. Saute about 3 minutes. Beat egg yolk with salt, tarragon, garlic and sour cream. Add to skillet. Cook until blended and bubbly. Add cheese. Heat until melted. Spoon into heated individual serving dishes. Sprinkle with parsley. Slice paté. Place slice on top of each dish. Serve immediately.

6 servings   4.6 gm. per serving

OIGNONS PARMESAN

These unusual onions taste almost like noodles. Try them with steak!

8 medium onions, sliced
1/4 cup butter
1/2 cup grated Parmesan cheese

164

Saute onions in butter 10 to 12 minutes. Remove to baking dish. Sprinkle cheese over top. Broil 5 inches from heat until cheese melts.

6 servings   13.5 gm. per serving

SAUTE OF SQUASH

3/4 lb. zucchini
3/4 lb. yellow crookneck squash
1 tbs. olive oil
1/2 tsp. garlic powder
1 tsp. onion powder
1/2 tsp. salt
pepper
1/2 cup (2 oz.) grated cheddar or Parmesan cheese

Wash squash. Grate diagonally on medium side of grater. Heat oil in heavy skillet. Add squash. Cook, covered, over medium heat until bottom of squash is brown. Turn with spatula. Add seasonings. Lower heat a little. Cook stirring frequently for 10 minutes or until tender. Add cheese. Lower heat. Cook until cheese melts.

4 servings   5 gm. per serving

FAVORITE SPINACH

2 bunches fresh spinach
5 slices bacon

Wash spinach several times. Drain. Dice bacon. Brown in large pot. Add washed spinach. Cover. Lower heat. Cook 6 minutes.

166

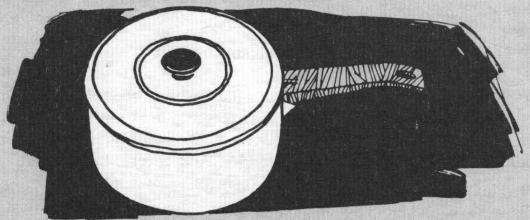

4 servings   3 gm. per serving

PARMESAN TOMATOES

These go well with many foods. Besides tasting so good, they add color and interest to meals.

2 whole ripe tomatoes
2 tbs. butter or mayonnaise
1/4 cup grated Parmesan cheese
2 tsp. minced parsley

167

Cut tomatoes in half. Mix remaining ingredients. Spread mixture on tomatoes. Broil 4 inches from heat until topping is crispy and lightly browned, about 5 minutes.

4 servings

2 gm. per serving

Desserts

Most diets forbid desserts, but the Low Carbohydrate Diet is the exception. Have whipped cream and strawberries, if you like, or Grand Marnier Souffle!

Except when having company, I personally feel it is better to curb one's sweet tooth and avoid desserts altogether. If you simply must have something sweet to "quit on," D-Zerta is a good choice.

When you do serve dessert, select one that meets the requirements set by the entree. A light dessert such as Daiquiri Chiffon goes with a heavy meal, or if the meal is light, choose something rich and creamy like Zabaglione.

Company will love these delectable desserts and no one will know there's a dieter in the crowd. All of these yummy concoctions should make for happy endings.

ANGEL PIE

A delectable, make ahead dessert for company. It must be refrigerated 24 hours before serving.

4 egg whites
1/2 tsp. cream of tartar
dash of salt
1 tsp. vanilla
1 cup Sugar Twin

Preheat oven to 275°F. Spray 12 inch pie tin with Pam. Beat egg whites until foamy. Add cream of tartar, salt and vanilla. Beat until stiff. Add Sugar Twin gradually. Beat until dissolved. Line pie tin with meringue. Keep it thick on the bottom and thin on the sides. Bake in preheated oven 1 hour. Turn heat off. Allow to dry in oven another 15 minutes. While meringue is baking, prepare filling.

8-12 servings   Trace gm. per serving

LEMON FILLING

4 egg yolks
1/2 cup Sugar Twin
1/8 tsp. salt
2 tbs. lemon juice
1/4 tsp. almond extract
2 cups (1 pt.) heavy cream, whipped

171

Beat egg yolks with Sugar Twin, salt and lemon juice. Cook over low heat until mixture is thick. Stir constantly. Remove from heat. Add almond extract. Chill. Fold half of whipped cream into cooled filling. Pour into meringue shell. Top with remaining cream. Refrigerate 24 hours or overnight before serving.

DAIQUIRI CHIFFON

This unique dessert is easy to prepare and very refreshing.

1 envelope unflavored gelatine
1/2 cup Sugar Twin
1 cup water
1/4 cup vodka
3 tbs. fresh lime juice

1 tsp. grated lime peel
green food coloring
3 egg whites
1/2 cup heavy cream, whipped
2 tbs. coconut for garnish

Combine gelatine and Sugar Twin in small saucepan. Stir in water. Heat just to boiling. Stir constantly. Blend in vodka, lime juice and peel. Add just enough food coloring to tint pale green. Chill until mixture reaches a syrupy consistency. Beat egg whites until stiff, but not dry. Fold gelatine mixture into whites. Carefully fold in whipped cream. Pour into 1 quart mold. Chill until firm. Unmold on serving plate. Garnish with coconut.

6 servings   1.1 gm. per serving

FLAMING RUM OMELET

Serve this light, delicate dessert after a heavy meal. It's very impressive.

1/4 cup butter, melted
4 eggs
1 packet Sugar Twin
dash salt
2 tbs. brown Sugar Twin
1/4 cup rum, warmed

Beat eggs, Sugar Twin and salt together thoroughly. Heat 3 tablespoons butter in omelet pan until bubbly. Pour in eggs. Stir gently with fork bringing the cooked egg at the edges of the pan into the center. When eggs are set and still creamy, roll up. Brush top with remaining melted butter. Sprinkle with brown Sugar Twin. Pour over warmed rum. Ignite and serve flaming.

2 servings   1.5 gm. per serving

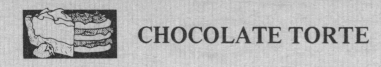 **CHOCOLATE TORTE**

Pretty to see, delicious to eat and can be made a day ahead.

6 egg whites
1/2 tsp. cream of tartar
1 tsp. almond extract

1-1/2 cups Sugar Twin
1/4 cup slivered almonds

Preheat oven to 300°F. Beat egg whites, cream of tartar and almond extract in a large mixing bowl until soft peaks form. Gradually add Sugar Twin. Continue beating until stiff. Spray cookie sheets with Pam. Spread meringue in three, 6-inch circles. Bake in preheated oven 25 minutes or until lightly browned. Remove from cookie sheets immediately. Cool. Place one layer on serving plate. Spread 1/3 of Chocolate Cream Filling on top. Add another layer and spread with 1/3 of filling. Continue until layers and filling are used. Sprinkle almonds over top. Refrigerate several hours or overnight.

10 servings   2.7 gm. per serving

CHOCOLATE CREAM FILLING

1/2 cup Sugar Twin
1/4 cup unsweetened cocoa
1/2 tsp. vanilla
1-1/2 cups heavy cream
1/4 cup cream de cacao

175

Combine Sugar Twin, cocoa, vanilla and cream in a small mixing bowl. Beat until thick. Add cream de cacao. Beat until stiff. Spread over meringue layers.

GRAND MARNIER SOUFFLE

A perfect dessert to delight your guests. They'll never guess you're on a diet!

6 cup souffle dish
2/3 cup Sugar Twin
5 eggs, separated
1 envelope unflavored gelatine

1/4 cup Grand Marnier
1 cup (1/2 pt.) heavy cream
dash salt
1/4 tsp. cream of tartar

Prepare souffle dish by adding a waxed paper or foil collar which extends 2 inches above dish. Heat Sugar Twin with 1/4 cup water. Beat egg yolks in large mixing bowl. Pour in syrup in a thin stream, beating constantly. Soften gelatine in 1/4 cup cold water 5 minutes. Heat until dissolved. Beat into egg yolks. Add Grand Marnier. Beat egg whites until foamy. Add cream of tartar and salt. Beat until stiff. Whip cream until it forms soft peaks. Fold into yolk mixture. Gently fold in stiffly beaten egg whites. Pour mixture into souffle dish. Refrigerate at least 2 hours. Overnight is even better. Remove collar before serving.

6 servings   2.3 gm. per serving

STRAWBERRIES WITH SOUR CREAM

1 quart fresh strawberries
1/2 cup brown Sugar Twin
1 cup (1/2 pint) sour cream

    Wash berries. Do not remove stems. Arrange on individual dessert plates with a mound of brown Sugar Twin. Put sour cream in a serving bowl. Dip berries in cream, then in brown Sugar Twin.

6 servings

8.6 gm. per serving

STRAWBERRIES CHANTILLY

If strawberries are your passion, you'll love these.

1 quart fresh strawberries
2 packets Sugar Twin
2 tbs. Kirsch
1 cup (1/2 pt.) whipping cream

Carefully wash strawberries. Save a few whole ones for garnish. Cut the remaining ones in half. Add Sugar Twin and Kirsch to cream. Whip until stiff. Fold in berries. Spoon into crystal goblets. Top with whole strawberries. Refrigerate 2 hours.

4 servings   9 gm. per serving

ZABAGLIONE

Italian Zabaglione is a beautiful way to end a meal. Spoon over blueberries for an extra touch, and enjoy.

6 egg yolks
1/3 cup Sugar Twin
1/3 cup Marsala or Sherry

Combine egg yolks and Sugar Twin in top of double boiler. Beat with a rotary beater until thick and foamy. Slowly add Marsala. Place over hot, not boiling, water. Beat constantly until thick and fluffy. Spoon into slender glasses.

4 servings   1.7 gm. per serving

Index

181